Fr Michael Dungan's Blanchardstown, 1836–1868

Maynooth Studies in Local History

SERIES EDITOR   Raymond Gillespie

This is one of six titles to be published in the Maynooth Studies in Local History series in 2002. The first forty titles were published by Irish Academic Press; the next volumes in the series are being published by Four Courts Press. The publication of this series is a reflection of the continued growth of interest in local and regional history within Ireland in recent years. That interest has manifested itself in diverse ways, including new research about the problems of local and regional societies in the past. These short books seek to make a contribution to that research. As in previous years most are drawn from theses completed as part of the MA in local history at NUI Maynooth.

The new studies published this year are concerned, as their predecessors have been, with the problem of how groups of people within relatively well-defined geographical contexts tried to resolve the problems presented by daily life in the past. Sometimes the areas studied may correspond to administrative units, sometimes not. One local society dealt with this year, Rossin, was an 'unofficial place', known as a distinct community only by those who lived there rather than by administrators. Even such unofficial places had problems in daily life. In some cases those problems had dramatic outcomes. Family jealousies over land and marriage could lead to murder. Elsewhere family networks shaped political actions during the land war. Although local historians are fascinated by the unusual and the violent the daily activities of ordinary life are equally important. The commonplace routines of making a living in an industrial town, worshipping at the local holy well in the way determined by local custom or in the parish church surrounded by one's neighbours are part of the story of the evolution of local societies and all are dealt with in this group of studies.

Taken together these new titles demonstrate yet again, if demonstration is still required, the vibrancy and diversity of the local societies which make up Ireland's past. In presenting this diversity to the modern world they also reveal the challenges which await other local historians to take up the stories of their own areas. In doing so they contribute to the lively discipline that local history has become in recent years.

Maynooth Studies in Local History: Number 42

Fr Michael Dungan's Blanchardstown, 1836–1868

Elizabeth Cronin

FOUR COURTS PRESS

Set in 10pt on 12pt Bembo by
Carrigboy Typesetting Services, County Cork for
FOUR COURTS PRESS LTD
Fumbally Lane, Dublin 8, Ireland
e-mail: info@four-courts-press.ie
http://www.four-courts-press.ie
and in North America for
FOUR COURTS PRESS
c/o ISBS, 5824 N.E. Hassalo Street, Portland, OR 97213.

© Elizabeth Cronin 2002

ISBN 1–85182–711–0

Printed in Ireland by
ColourBooks Ltd, Dublin

Contents

Acknowledgements

I wish to acknowledge with gratitude some of the many people who helped me to complete this study: Professor R.V. Comerford and the Department of Modern History, NUI Maynooth; the course director, Dr Raymond Gillespie, for his help and encouragement; my supervisor, Dr Thomas O'Connor for his valuable advice, guidance and practical assistance; the Very Revd Walter Harris PP, Blanchardstown; Ms Kathleen Somers; Sister Immaculata, Prioress, Monastery of the Incarnation, Drumcondra; Fr Thomas Davitt, Archivist, and Fr Myles Reardon, Assistant Archivist, St Paul's Raheny; Sister Terence, Archivist, Dominican Convent Cabra; Fr Philip Deane OFM Multyfarnham; the Very Revd Dermot Clarke.

My thanks to: John Danaher, Ordnance Survey, Phoenix Park; Paul Ferguson, Map Library, Trinity College; William Brennan, present owner of the building which was formerly St Brigid's Academy, and his associate Oliver Beirne; David Sheehy, Archivist, Dublin Diocesan Archives; Richard Farrell and staff, Blanchardstown Public Library; Penny Woods and staff, Russell Library, Maynooth; the staffs of the National Library, National Archives, NUI Maynooth and the Representative Church Body Library; my colleagues in the MA class Maynooth; my family and friends who entered into the project with me. Finally, and especially, my mother and Maureen, without whose support this study could not have been completed.

Introduction

I have important news. We have appointed the Revd Mr Dungan to the vacant parish of Blanchardstown and he has thankfully accepted it.'[1] So wrote the vicar general of the Dublin diocese, Dr Meyler, to Dean Hamilton on 23 September 1836. This was very important news indeed for the people of Blanchardstown. For the next 32 years this parish priest played a central role in the life of the Catholic parish of St Brigid, Blanchardstown.

This study sets out to examine and attempts to reconstruct the parish as it was in the period of that pastorate, 1836–68. Fr Dungan kept a diary which is preserved in the archives of St Brigid's Church Blanchardstown. This diary in conjunction with account books, altar books and a confraternity book are the principal primary sources which form the basis of this work. In addition to these sources I also had access to the Convent book of the Carmelite nuns whose foundation in Blanchardstown broadly coincides with the period being examined.[2] This book is a chronicle of all the events which the nuns regarded as important both in their own community and in the parish. Fr Thomas McNamara, a Vincentian priest who was in Castleknock College between 1835 and 1837, wrote his memoirs in 1867.[3] There are several references in these memoirs to the involvement of the Vincentians in the parish during the pastorate of Fr Joy Dean in the early nineteenth century. Both the convent book and the memoirs corroborate, highlight and in some cases give a different perspective on the principal source – the diary.

Other sources have been used in order to draw a picture of the Blanchardstown of the mid-nineteenth century. Census reports, agricultural statistics, application forms to the National Board of Education for aid, as well as inspectors' reports all combine to create a picture of a west Co. Dublin parish at this time. While the census reports give a profile of the type of housing in the parish and an insight into living conditions, the visitation reports compiled for the archbishop's visits indicate the poverty of both church and people at this time. These reports show how basic the church was in terms of its physical structures, its devotional life and the paucity of liturgical vessels and vestments in the first thirty years of the nineteenth century.[4]

The diary has been central to the work. It is a record of all that Fr Dungan perceived to be important. Every facet of his life is covered; his comings and his goings; the names of those he entertains and those who entertain him. He buys and sells animals. He plants and harvests crops. He records all his activities in trying to raise money for chapels and schools, he records the charity sermons, who preached them and how much they raised. The juxtaposition of the entries shows how 'seamlessly' the parish priest saw his world. Attendance at the funeral mass of Archbishop Murray is found side by side with the 'boarding' of Porterstown chapel, the visit of the countess of Clarendon to Blanchardstown and an almost audible sigh of relief that 'the masons are done at the side of the [parochial] house after nine weeks'.[5]

This diary as in the case of all diaries is 'subjective'. W.G. Hoskins believes that 'the value of old diaries cannot be over-estimated, though the deficiencies of such material will be obvious enough'.[6] He points out that because diaries are 'unofficial' they probably reflect more of the truth than an official document.[7] However, Hoskins warns that because the diarist is likely to be giving a highly subjective impression of an event or a person, such records should be treated 'with proper caution and reservations'.[8] In the case of this particular study, the supporting contemporaneous sources serve to correct any imbalance and so the diary can be used to reconstruct the Blanchardstown of Fr Michael Dungan.

Several studies have been done on this west Dublin area in the last twenty years. *Cnucha, a history of Castleknock*, by James O'Driscoll was published in 1977. In the author's own words, he 'decided to pay more attention to Castleknock itself because of the important position it held through the centuries right back to the time of the Fianna'.[9] Blanchardstown merits only four pages, and the perspective is on secular history. Charles and Mary Hulgraine's *St Mochta's Church, Porterstown. A local history*, published in 1990 to mark the centenary of St Mochta's Church, concentrated on the immediate Porterstown area with very little reference to the original nineteenth-century parish. *A history of St Brigid's Church, Blanchardstown, 1837–1987*, was compiled by the then parish priest of Blanchardstown, the late Fr Séamus McGeehan, Pat Kelly, and Catherine Cullen, but never published. It was circulated to the parishioners who attended the 150th anniversary Mass in St Brigid's on Sunday, 1 November 1987. This booklet charts the development of the Catholic parish of Blanchardstown from its emergence from the penal times to the present. As it was written with the actual anniversary celebration in mind there is a strong emphasis on the role of Fr Joy Dean as the person who laid the foundation of the church and to whose plan Fr Dungan built it.[10] Fr Joy Dean's Presbyterian relatives and his Catholic Franciscan great-grand-nephew were all present as well as the local members of the other religious denominations in the area. Sadly none of Fr Dungan's relatives were present and he got scant mention on the day.[11] However the booklet does correct the balance and Fr Dungan's trojan work in the parish is acknowledged. Within the confines of the 62 pages of the booklet, the diary can get no more than a brief mention.

This study is divided into three parts. The first chapter deals with Fr Dungan's Blanchardstown. It locates the parish and notes its topographical and demo-graphic dimensions. It examines the economic situation and the means of livelihood of the parishioners. To set the scene for the appointment of Fr Dungan it was necessary to look at the pastorates of his immediate predecessors, Fathers Miles McPharlan and Joseph Joy Dean.

The second chapter examines the church building/renovation programmes of Fr Dungan and notes particularly how he involved so many parishioners in these activities. The ability of the parish priest to delegate and to enable the many committees to function effectively becomes very clear in this chapter. The many devotional practices initiated or introduced by the parish priest are examined. The practice of visiting the many holy wells in the parish is discussed. The introduction of novenas to wean the parishioners from the pattern and to draw them into more church-centred devotions is also considered here. In the same way the function of the Purgatorian Society encouraged by the parish priest marks an attempt to curb the practices which surrounded the traditional Irish wake.

The third chapter examines the role of education, especially primary education in the parish. It deals with the building and renovation of schools. It is in the area of education that a sectarian dimension is most evident. Fr Dungan, like Fr Joy Dean before him became embroiled in controversy with the Protestant headmaster in Porterstown national school.[12] While there was conflict there was also co-operation, due in no small way to the personalities of the two protagonists, the Revd Ralph Sadlier, rector of Castleknock, and Fr Michael Dungan, parish priest of Blanchardstown.

This ability to work harmoniously with people was one of Fr Dungan's great gifts and was appreciated by his parishioners as was his long pastorate of service. This was shown clearly on the day of his funeral.

> At 11 a.m. on Saturday 8 February 1868 every part of the Church set apart for the laity was crowded by a congregation which had come to offer up their prayers to the throne of grace for the everlasting rest of the soul of the good pastor who had lived and died in the service of God and his people. At the end of the mass the remains were borne on the shoulders of the people in procession around the exterior of the sacred edifice as the clergy chanted the psalms prescribed by the ritual for such occasions. The funeral returned to the church and after the last prayers were intoned the remains were lowered into the vault in the centre of the choir. This was a holy and venerable priest who closed his days amidst the harvest of his good works and whose name shall be held in benediction by the poor whom he relieved, the ignorant whom he instructed, the sinners whom he converted – by all whom he edified by the sanctity of his honoured life.[13]

The parishioners of St Brigid's commemorated Fr Dungan in the very year of his death by putting into the church a stained glass window[14] and beneath this window a marble plaque was inserted in the masonry of the wall.[15] But perhaps more important monuments are the churches and schools which Fr Dungan built and the sense of community which he helped to create in the course of his 32-year pastorate in Blanchardstown.

1. Fr Dungan's Blanchardstown

The period 1836–68 was a formative time in the life of the Catholic parish of St Brigid, Blanchardstown. This study sets out to identify changes in the parish in the period and to see these changes as a microcosm of what was happening in the archdiocese of Dublin and in the country as a whole.

The Catholic Church as it emerged from the eighteenth century found a new confidence which was expressed in the open expansion of services at institutional, structural, liturgical and personnel level. The Church authorities now had the opportunity to implement the Tridentine reform which saw the parish as the basic unit of ecclesiastical organization and the priest as the central figure within the parish.[1] The new parish priest of Blanchardstown in 1836, Fr Michael Dungan, fitted perfectly into this role. On 29 October 1836, he was inducted into the parish, succeeding Fr Joy Dean who had died on 26 July having spent over 34 years in the parish, both as curate and parish priest.[2] There is a significant contrast between the pastorate of Fr Dungan and that of his predecessor, due in part to their different backgrounds, spiritual formation and especially their personalities. Joy Dean was born in Belfast about 1752, to a Protestant mother and Catholic father.[3] He was educated and ordained on the continent where he remained until his appointment as curate to Blanchardstown in 1802.[4] He was involved for many years in the academic worlds of Lisbon and Salamanca and used this educational experience when he established St Brigid's Academy in Blanchardstown in 1810 (fig. 1).[5] This establishment was 'designed for the education of young gentlemen' and offered a range of languages which included Portuguese, French, German, Spanish, Latin and Greek.[6] Fr Joy Dean himself conducted 'lectures on experimental philosophy'[7]. He combined the roles of president of this academy and curate until his appointment as parish priest in December 1825.[8]

Joy Dean lived and worked through the last days of the Mass-rock. He saw the slackening of the penal laws and the coming of Emancipation in 1829. He experienced the changing status of the Catholic priest from *persona non grata* to government-approved manager and patron of schools under the National Board of Education. So, by the time of his death, the status of the priest in Ireland had changed dramatically. The Catholic Church had moved from being a grudgingly tolerated organization to being an accepted part of the structures of power and influence within Irish society.[9]

While Fr Joy Dean came out of the European tradition, the influences on Fr Dungan were wholly Irish, strongly marked by a Maynooth formation. In many ways, he symbolized the new mood of freedom and openness to change

1 The building that housed St Brigid's Academy, Blanchardstown.

that characterised the nineteenth century. He was born in Dublin in 1799, entered Maynooth at the age of nineteen and was ordained on 24 May 1823.[10] He was the first parish priest of Blanchardstown to be educated and ordained in Maynooth.[11] He could be described as a typical priest of his time, a 'new man'. One can follow the progress of the century through the events of his life, all aspects of which were open to the 'progressive' spirit of the age. He was a broker and agent of change in the parish for the next 32 years.

Fr Dungan's death notice stated that 'the late Archbishop marked his appreciation of Fr Dungan's merits by appointing him to the vacant parish of Blanchardstown'.[12] Given the circumstances in St Brigid's from 1802 to 1836, it is very likely that this appointment was a very considered and calculated move on the part of Daniel Murray, archbishop of Dublin (1823–52). The new parish priest required just the qualities possessed by Fr Dungan to heal the divisions which existed in the parish and the sense of alienation which was expressed in a petition from the parishioners of St Brigid's to Archbishop Murray 10 years earlier in April 1826.[13] This petition, signed by 702 parishioners, was regarded by them as something which could only 'be justified by the most paramount necessity'. They requested Dr Murray to 'institute an inquiry among the laity, who complained of a system of neglect unexampled in any other parish in the diocese. This neglect, according to the parishioners, arose from the many changes of curates and 'from the unfortunate circumstances of the Revd Gentleman over them having devoted himself to temporal concerns, by which he became a stranger in his own parish and lost the respect which is necessary between pastor and flock'.[14] This section of the petition refers to Fr Miles McPharlan, Fr Joy Dean's predecessor who was parish priest of Blanchardstown from 1802 to 1825.[15] Most of his pastorate was spent in Douglas, Isle of Man, where he fled to avoid imprisonment for debts incurred when a parish venture failed.[16] On 2 December 1825 Fr McPharlan was deprived of his title to the parish of Blanchardstown by Archbishop Murray.[17] On the same day Fr Joy Dean was appointed parish priest of Blanchardstown, 'vacant by reason of M. McPharlan's contumacious absence'.[18]

Fr McPharlan was regarded very highly in Douglas where he established the first post-Reformation church on the island in 1814.[19] It seems extraordinary that despite his financial difficulties in Blanchardstown he was able to build 'through the aid of his friends in Ireland a commodious place of Divine Worship'.[20] He did this without being 'canonically sent, appointed, nor facultied'.[21] This 'missionary' labour of their parish priest was clearly not appreciated by his parishioners back home! With the appointment of Joy Dean, they viewed the prospect of yet another 'absentee' parish priest with alarm. They believed that his presidency of St Brigid's Academy, Blanchardstown would continue to be his priority.[22] The parishioners 'felt doomed to their former situation by having a pastor over them who, like his predecessor was involved in temporal concerns'.[23]

This petition had an immediate impact. Fr Joy Dean closed the Academy, whether voluntarily or by order of the archbishop, cannot be established. He invited the Carmelite nuns to take it over, which they did in June 1828.[24] From 1826 on, Fr Joy Dean became totally involved in the running of the parish. In 1829 he took a parish census 'going from house to house to ascertain exactly how far his jurisdiction and obligations extended, to know his flock and make them know their pastor'.[25] After spending twenty-seven years in the parish it does seem extraordinary that he was only getting to know his parishioners at this point.

Fr Joy Dean was 73 years old when he was appointed parish priest of St Brigid's.[26] His continental background, his academic leanings, his patriarchal air and manner and his tendency to frequently express himself in Latin must have created a barrier between priest and people, even though his death notice paints a slightly different picture:[27]

> Characterised by the highest polish and amenity of manners he could move in the first circles of society with ease and dignity and at the same time feel, and make himself at home among the poorest of his people.[28]

It is against this background that 37-year-old Fr Michael Dungan took up his appointment to Blanchardstown on 13 October 1836.[29] The 1826 petition showed how concerned the parishioners were for the presence of a full-time parish priest. This augured well for the pastorate of Fr Dungan. It is interesting to note that within a very short time, many of the 702 parishioners who had signed the petition were actively involved in the many committees set up by the new parish priest. They came from all areas of the parish right across the social spectrum. For example, among the signatories were James Halpin, owner of the Blanchardstown Mill, the biggest employer in the parish and his wife Anne, who became helpers and close friends of Fr Dungan. Another signatory James Reilly was always available to travel with Fr Dungan to Longford, Cork and Limerick or to carry out maintenance of the parochial house with his men. Mr Fitzpatrick too accompanied the parish priest to Liverpool and spent eleven days with him collecting for the building of the new church in Chapelizod. George Warren became a church collector and eventually, president of the Confraternity of the Christian Doctrine. Two other signatories, Matt Kenna and Philip Leckin, were helped by Fr Dungan when the former was in prison and the latter involved in a court case. At the other end of the social scale, Christy Cootes who signed the petition with an X, got employment from Dungan cutting the hay and reaping the corn on the eight and a half acres of land attached to the parochial house. Christy Cootes also lived in one of the three cottages which Fr Dungan had built on his land. Mary Thornton who lived at the 12th lock of the Royal Canal which passed through Blanchardstown and another signatory of the petition had a very different relationship with Fr Dungan than she had with his predecessor. Mary and Fr Dungan were obviously on such friendly terms that she gave him cures and remedies which he thought worth recording in his diary.[30]

Fr Dungan kept a diary which is now preserved with account books and confraternity books in the archives of St Brigid's Church. The diary consists of a ledger containing 85 pages of perfectly legible script. From this diary it is possible to construct a chronicle of important milestones in the development of the Church in Blanchardstown. It provides a series of snapshots of this west Dublin community and brings to life the daily concerns of a parish priest in a changing rural parish, just six miles from the centre of Dublin, in the pre-Famine and post-Famine period. It is possible to see this Blanchardstown community as a 'distinct articulation' of national life but with its own peculiar features.[31]

The parish which emerges from the pages of the diary was fairly self-sufficient. It had a strong agricultural base. Fr Dungan was a full-time 'hands on' parish priest who spoke the language of the people, the language of cattle, crops and weather He seemed to balance very effectively the spiritual and temporal needs of his people. The parish of St Brigid covered a very large area, stretching from the Liffey at Islandbridge to Lucan, Luttrellstown and the Meath border. It included the Phoenix Park and Cabra[32] (fig. 2). The main

1 St Brigid's Church.
2 St Brigid's Seminary later Carmelite Convent.
3 Chapelizod Church.
4 Porterstown Church.
5 Kellystown Church & School now site of Scout's Den
6 Clonsilla Church
7 Cloghran Graveyard.
8 Dominican Convent Cabra.
9 Coemhin Graveyard Abbots.
10 Mulhuddart Graveyard.
11 Lady's Well.
12 Rag Well Diswellstown.
13 Rag Well Darby's Hill.
14 Pound Hill Luttrelstown.
15 Luttrelstown Castle.
16 Dunsink Observatory.

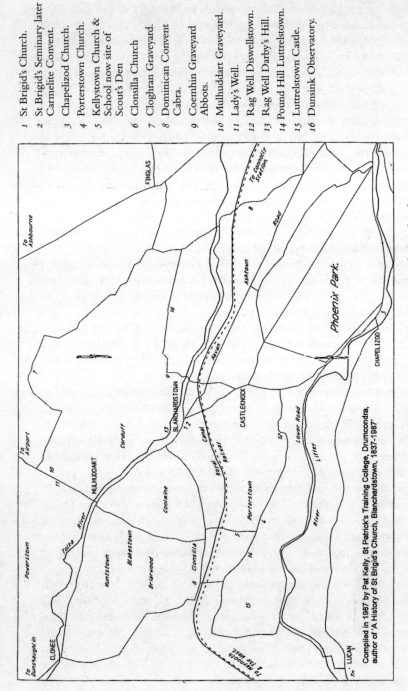

2 Map of nineteenth-century Catholic parish of Blanchardstown.

Compiled in 1987 by Pat Kelly, St Patrick's Training College, Drumcondra, author of 'A History of St Brigid's Church, Blanchardstown, 1837–1987'

church and parish priest's house were located in the village of Blanchardstown. There were two chapels of ease, one in Porterstown and the other in Chapelizod.[33] In the early years of his pastorate, Fr Dungan had only one curate, Fr Laurence Carty and they both serviced the three chapels.[34] At this time there were four public Masses every Sunday: two in Blanchardstown, one in Porterstown and one in Chapelizod.[35] It was estimated that in Blanchardstown 300 people attended the first Mass and almost 700 assisted at the second Mass.[36] By the time of Fr Dungan's death there were three curates in the parish.[37] The increased number of curates reflects the improved supply of priests and also the rise in population in the parish.

In 1836, the parish was well served by the Dominican and Carmelite nuns and by the Vincentian priests. Fr Dungan's nearest neighbours were the Carmelite nuns in the Convent of the Incarnation located directly across from the parochial house and beside the church. This foundation was made in Blanchardstown in 1828 in response to a request from Fr Joy Dean to Dr Daniel Murray, archbishop of Dublin.[38] There were only four sisters in the original community, but by Fr Dungan's time the number had increased to 13.[39] They had purchased the former Academy from Fr Joy Dean for £700, using the dowry of the first novice in Blanchardstown, Teresa McDonnell for the purpose.[40] The strict contemplative life laid down by the Carmelite rule was not observed in Ireland at this time as it was felt that the nuns were needed to work in Catholic education.[41] The Blanchardstown Carmelites opened a school for the poor girls of the area which they financed by establishing a boarding school in the old Academy building.[42] The Carmelites were involved in the parish not only as teachers but also through their spiritual ministry of prayer and intercession for the local community.[43]

At the Cabra end of the parish, the Dominican nuns were similarly involved since 1819 in teaching and providing for the local poor.[44] By 1846 the Dominicans had also set up the first Catholic institute for deaf girls in Ireland.[45] They were guided in this by the Vincentian priest, Thomas McNamara, one of the founding fathers of Castleknock College, who took over the running of St Peter's Church, Phibsborough, in 1838 when it was handed over to the Vincentians by Archbishop Murray.[46]

The parish of Blanchardstown was home to the Vincentian community who had established a boarding school for boys at St Vincent's, Castleknock in 1835.[47] From the outset, the priests of Castleknock made a valuable contribution to the life of the parish. Their role in catechesis and evangelisation will be discussed later in this study.

There were also three Protestant churches in the parish: St Brigid's in Castleknock, St Mary's in Clonsilla, and St Laurence's in Chapelizod.[48] Morgan's school for boys and Mercer's school for girls, both situated in the same complex in Ashtown, catered for the education of the local Church of Ireland children.[49]

Fr Dungan's pastorate saw some demographic changes in St Brigid's parish. Its population in 1841 was 9,855.[50] This rose to 10,206 in 1851.[51] The parish was in the barony of Castleknock and covered much the same area, comprising about 15,539 acres.[52] Despite the size of the Blanchardstown parish it was not viewed by Fr Dungan's fellow priests as a desirable appointment.[53] However, the poverty of the parish did not deter the parish priest of Kilquade, Fr Charles Stennett from angling for this appointment.[54] He urged Fr Woods to plead his cause with the archbishop. Stennett believed that he was not looking for a promotion in coming back to Blanchardstown where he began his ministry as a curate.[55] In fact he was leaving a far better thing (Kilquade) in the gift of his Grace.[56] Charles Stennett was English and a widower who was ordained in 1814.[57] How did he come to be a curate in Blanchardstown? Was he involved in the Academy with Fr Joy Dean? Interestingly, one of the reasons he gave for wishing to return to Blanchardstown was to enjoy the company of Mr Dowley and his community, and Andrew Rorke.[58] He had 'not a soul to commune with in Kilquade' and he wanted to escape from the Orangemen who he claimed lived there.[59] Despite his begging the archbishop to keep him in mind he was not appointed to Blanchardstown.[60]

In the same letter, Fr Woods, of the Pro-Cathedral, wrote to Dean Hamilton, Archbishop Murray's secretary, that 'conjecture is not very high nor busy about the vacated living of Blanchardstown. It is considered no better than a curacy'.[61] According to Fr Woods, 'whoever got Blanchardstown would have a great deal of trouble for Betty [Fr Dean's housekeeper] lorded it over the parish and did as she pleased with the dues'.[62] Betty, apparently, was still in possession of the parochial house three months after the death of Fr Joy Dean, and 'she had lived last month on the collections from the chapel door'. Fr Woods believed that, 'bella, horrida bella' would have to be the new parish priest's motto.[63]

Fr Dungan, however, was not bellicose. In fact he was seen as a priest of 'great humility and gentle manners'.[64] He appears to have achieved a *modus vivendi* with Betty who stayed on in the parochial house and actually outlived him.[65] There were other more pressing problems than the domestic. The big task facing Fr Dungan was to continue the infrastructural work his predecessor had begun. The present church of St Brigid was in the process of construction when he was appointed.[66] It was a mere shell with £100 owing to the builder.[67] Fr Carty gave him £4 – the total amount in the parish fund in 1836.[68] The existing schools had to be refurbished and new schools built. An eminently practical man, Fr Dungan first addressed himself to the financial challenge. Rising above sentiment, he had Fr Joy Dean's silver spoons raffled and raised £30 towards the parish debt.[69] Indeed, this raffle could be seen as symbolic of the man. Despite his business acumen and perhaps because of it, he was often insolvent and raffles raised money reasonably quickly. It was spoons in 1836, a pony in 1856 and a silver snuff box in 1863.[70] In 1866, just two years before his death, he raffled his wristwatch, worth £12, and raised

£94.19s. 3d., all of which went towards the building of a new school in Blanchardstown village.[71] Interestingly, in this instance, he did not have to part with his watch as the lady who won it, Miss Connolly of Dalkey, elected to take £10 in lieu so he made a profit of £73. 10s. 2d. (after raffle expenses were cleared) and retained his watch.[72]

Infrastructural activity was only a part of Fr Dungan's ministry. His main concern was to draw the Catholic community closer to the church as the centre of parish worship. To this end he set up programmes of catechesis and evangelisation to deepen the devotional life of his parishioners. This was achieved by the formation of confraternities and sodalities.[73] Even when he was deeply involved in fundraising campaigns, he always pointed out that financial contributions were an expression and reflection of parishioners' faith.[74]

In both the infrastructural and pastoral challenges, Fr Dungan could rely on the local religious communities. For catechesis he was assisted by the local Vincentian community, who directed the Confraternity of Christian Doctrine as well as giving catechism classes and conducting parish missions.[75] The role of the Carmelite and Dominican nuns has already been mentioned. It could be argued that the high profile of religion and church affairs in the parish created a climate which facilitated Fr Dungan in setting up committees to assist his parish development plans. Local factory owners, like James Halpin, owner of the woollen mill beside the canal in Blanchardstown, and Bernard McGarry, who owned an oil factory in Ashtown, were Fr Dungan's constant helpers and advisors.[76] Farmers in the area such as the Simpsons of Elmgreen and the Hoeys of Buzzardstown were on many committees in the parish and these people involved their factory workers and labourers who also made financial contributions to the various parish projects.[77] Fr Dungan's ability to see the value of collaborative ministry facilitated this huge lay involvement during his pastorate and in turn, made him a very effective and a much loved and respected leader of the Catholic community in the parish of Blanchardstown.[78] It was probably the combination of these factors which blossomed and bore rich fruit in all areas of the community in the years 1836–68.

In 1801, farming in the Blanchardstown area was described as 'an advanced science'.[79] John O'Donovan confirmed this in 1836, the very year that Fr Dungan came to Blanchardstown. O'Donovan described the parish as 'generally flat with equal portions of tillage and pasture and having a highly cultivated appearance'.[80] This, however, was not the full picture. Side by side with the big houses and the strong farmers was great poverty. This poverty is reflected in the entries in Fr Dungan's diary, in the type of housing shown in the census returns and in the replies to the Poor Law Inquiry 1836. In 1841, just five years into Fr Dungan's pastorate, the census returns underline the poverty of Blanchardstown expressed in the type of housing. Thirty-five per cent of the population were living in fourth class housing – these were cabins mostly of mud and with only one room.[81] Thirty-two per cent lived in third-class housing which was only marginally better with two to four rooms and windows.[82]

In 1836, the Revd George O'Connor, rector of Castleknock, responding to the Commission of Inquiry into Poverty in the area reported that there were 100 widows and 300 children with no relatives to support them who were assisted from the parish fund.[83] One hundred persons were listed as unable to work due to old age or infirmity.[84] Mr William Thompson who answered the questionnaire on Mulhuddart stated that most cabins were made of clay and that the common diet was 'coarse wheat bread and potatoes'.[85] According to Mr Thompson, a labourer could expect to earn £18 to £20 per year, and women and children were 'a good deal employed', earning from 6*d*. to 8*d*. per day.[86] He went on to state that some of the labourers put money in the 'flourishing' savings bank, encouraged by their employers, while many more may have put their money into the thirteen public houses recorded by the Revd O'Connor.[87] The impression of the parish given by both O'Connor and Thompson is a favourable one, but it is unlikely that either one of them, given their positions, would wish to highlight the poverty which existed in the area. At the end of his submission, the Revd O'Connor stated that the district was 'very peaceable' with most of the poor 'contented with their lot'.[88]

Fr Dungan's diary contains very detailed lists of the poor of the parish who received a share of the lord lieutenant's Christmas charity at the viceregal lodge.[89] The extent of this poverty can be seen by looking at one entry in the diary. In 1852 the amount of the charity was £121 8*s*. Out of this money, sixty-four women, six girls, six boys and 12 men received blankets, rugs, bedgowns and linsey petticoats, shifts and flannel petticoats, cloaks, suits, shirts and flannel waistcoats.[90] Fr Dungan noted individual circumstances after the name of each recipient of the charity. Widows were in the majority. He also noted instances when persons whom he had judged eligible refused charity. In one particular case a widow came and took her daughter out of the queue at the viceregal lodge.[91] Equally, there were those who appeared to abuse the system, but Fr Dungan checked very carefully. He sometimes found that people who were on the Blanchardstown list also got themselves on the Castleknock list and one particular lady who was listed for a rug, succeeded in securing for herself a shift and flannel petticoat as well.[92] Presumably, she would be watched carefully the following year! There is a record in the diary also of soup being given out to the poor at the viceregal lodge, but this was only recorded for one year – 1852.[93] It is interesting to note that it was clothing and not food that was dispensed on a regular basis in the parish. Poverty rather than hunger seemed to be the prevailing problem. Nevertheless, Castleknock Dispensary quoted instances where actual disease had been brought on by want of proper sustenance as well as by inadequate clothes and bedding.[94]

The parish priest was no stranger to poverty. He had spent the previous ten years of his curacy in the parish of St Catherine in the Dublin Liberties.[95]

This was a useful experience and a kind of apprenticeship in how to provide for the religious, educational, and the ordinary material needs of a large parish on very limited resources. He was only too familiar with poor housing, overcrowding, chronic poverty and endemic disease. However, the quiet rural village of Blanchardstown was very different from the densely populated Meath Street.

Economic activity in the parish was varied, though dominated by agriculture. In 1841, out of a population of 9,855 for the barony of Castleknock, 1,116 were employed in agriculture while 451 were employed in manufacturing and trades.[96] Most of the local men worked as farm labourers, cattle drovers and market gardeners.[97] During the building of the Dublin to Navan Turnpike road approximately 20 local men were employed in 1836.[98] The women were employed as domestic servants in the big houses around the area.[99] There was the woollen mill in Blanchardstown village, which gave employment to between 80 and 100 workers, male and female, at any one time.[100] In Fr Dungan's time, this factory was owned by James Halpin, already referred to, who figured prominently in parish fundraising committees. Another of Fr Dungan's stalwarts, Bernard McGarry, owned an oil factory in Ashtown and gave employment to local men.[101] James Tyrell had a factory in Pelletstown which manufactured shovels, spades and railings.[102] This factory provided employment for 16 workers in the summer and 10 in winter.[103] Chapelizod was the most industrialized area of the parish.[104] By 1837, Mr Crosthwaite had 600 workers in his flax mill in Chapelizod.[105] All of these industries as well as giving employment opened up the area to outside influences.

The Rathborne family who had the candle factory in Dunsinea were neighbours of Fr Dungan. They were good employers and very involved in their own church, the Church of Ireland, in Castleknock.[106] Rathbornes were major suppliers of candles to churches of both denominations in both Ireland and England.[107] Fr Dungan was one of their customers.[108] While he was on 'buying' terms with the Rathbornes, he was on dining terms with Mr Crosthwaite, another Church of Ireland factory owner in Chapelizod.[109] So, what was reported of Westmeath in 1839 that priests no longer dined in the houses of Protestants is certainly not true of Blanchardstown in the same period.[110] Fr Dungan must have been aware that the employment given to his parishioners by people like the Rathbornes and the Crosthwaites had to be acknowledged and even reciprocated in the case of the candles being bought from Rathbornes.

Was this occupational diversity and the variety of crops cultivated in what was essentially a market garden area one of the reasons that the Famine did not significantly affect Blanchardstown? There are no direct references to the Famine in the diary. In 1846, Fr Dungan's dairy was broken into and a quantity of meal stolen.[111] One wonders if this were famine-related. There are no papers from the Castleknock barony among the Relief Commission papers in the National Archives, but in the vestry account books for the Church of Ireland parish of Castleknock, there are references to coffins provided for the poor of the parish between 1844 and 1847.[112] Coffins were costed at 4s. 9d.[113] In one day alone in 1847 there were seven burials in St Brigid's churchyard, Castleknock.[114]

Nor did the national trend of population decrease between 1841 and 1851 significantly affect Blanchardstown village.[115] Its demographic pattern was different. There, the relatively large decrease occurring between 1831 and 1841 showed up in the 1841 census returns.[116] The population declined from sixty-one families to thirty-four and from 343 persons to 182.[117] This was due to the cholera epidemic of the early 1830s when there were 119 cases between April 1832 and September 1833.[118] While cholera was no respector of age or social status, it took its toll particularly on the poor. A grant was given to Castleknock Dispensary to

> … defray expenses which must necessarily be incurred in a district of over 30 square miles, in cleansing, whitewashing and purifying the houses of the poor, removing nuisances, providing assistance, procuring conveyances for the removal of patients to hospital and in affording aids and nourishment for the poor to check the spread of contagion.[119]

Despite the poverty of these people, the backbone of the Catholic community, Fr Dungan was able to inspire them to contribute financially over many years for the support of ongoing church and school building. Even though he understood and sympathised with their poverty, he sought their involvement, which surely must have given them a sense of dignity and worth, encouraging them to contribute a penny or even a halfpenny on a regular basis.[120]

It is the rural character of Blanchardstown which emerges from the pages of Fr Dungan's diary. The buying and selling of animals, the harvesting of crops and the weather conditions were of real importance to his life. In 1844 the old cow house and the stable were thrown down by Mr Reilly and his men and a temporary stable erected.[121] By 1851, he had replaced the old dairy beside the hall door of the parochial house with a new dairy.[122] In June 1841, he wrote with obvious satisfaction that there was a very heavy meadow in the large field. Christy Cootes, one of his workmen commenced reaping the oats on 30 August 1845.[123]

In Fr Dungan's Blanchardstown, the horse reigned supreme and there are many references to horse power in the diary. Fr Dungan travelled around the parish on foot or on horseback. When he attended the seventeen victims drowned in the canal disaster on 25 November 1845, he travelled across the fields on horseback.[124] On the occasions when he went to conferences or into Dublin he used the pony and trap and he often brought his neighbouring priests from St Vincent's Castleknock with him.[125] If he wished to travel further, he could catch a 'fly' boat near the twelfth lock of the Royal Canal which ran from east to west through the parish.[126]

From the opening of the Midland Great Western Railway line through Blanchardstown in 1846, Fr Dungan travelled by rail to Dalkey, Bray and even to such far-flung places as Longford, Limerick and Cork.[127] He had at least one holiday in London and Paris. Accompanied by friends, William and Joseph Dirham, he left Dublin on 18 July 1851 and returned on 5 August.[128] The addresses at which they stayed in London and Paris are recorded in the diary. The round trip cost £15 each.[129]

The roads were not accident-free in the pre-motor car era as is shown by entries in the diary. On 19 June 1856, Fr Dungan went to the dedication of Rathmines new chapel.[130] On the way, he was in a collision on George's Street and he effectively wrote off his little car.[131] Ten days later, he had ordered a new car which Mr Cannon of Swords made for £12.[132] The new car, complete with cushions and lamps which cost an extra £1.7s., was collected by his workman/driver, Pat O'Brien from Swords on 10 October.[133] One can almost sense the parish priest's satisfaction as he recorded the total payment of £13.7s., to Mr Cannon in December 1856.[134] The accident in George's Street was not the only one. On 8 December 1845, his mare fell at Baron Lodge and bruised Fr Dungan's knee.[135] The injury must have put him out of action for at least a week as Fr Lynch of St Vincent's had to say Mass for him in Chapelizod on 14 December.[136] Dr Dirham, a personal friend applied leeches to the very bruised knee.[137] Pat O'Brien had an accident on 30 November while he was driving over Carlisle Bridge.[138] On another occasion, Betty was thrown from a jaunting car in Pill Lane.[139] One wonders was this fairly typical of the time, or were Pat and Fr Dungan speeding or accident prone. All these accidents occurred on roads which had been greatly improved in the period from 1836 onwards.[140]

At any one time, Fr Dungan had a mare and a horse.[141] As there were no fairs in Blanchardstown, he often went over the border to Dunboyne in Co. Meath to buy and sell both horses and cattle. On 15 August 1845, he went to Dunboyne with Mr Dunne to sell a horse he had bought from Walter Dungan, possibly a relative, and buy a new one.[142] He was no stranger to horses as the following year he went all the way to Rathfarnham fair where he bought another horse for £11.[143] The importance of the pony and cart as a means of transport for both goods and people is again underlined by an entry in the Carmelite Convent book for May 1844, when Mr O'Mara, a local farmer, presented the nuns with a pony and cart to bring their necessaries out from town.[144]

Fr Dungan's rural expertise extended beyond the equine. He bought and sold cattle as well as horses. On 22 November 1845, he went to Ratoath fair and sold a bullock and a yearling for £13.[145] On 1 July 1846, he bought a yearling cow from Christopher Kearns for £5.[146] Was he replacing the black cow that died of the distemper after nine or ten days of illness, on 4 October 1845?[147]

On 13 May 1856, he sent a cow and bullock to grass and on 1 October he sent a cow to Smithfield and got home one near to calving.[148] While the keeping of pigs is not mentioned in the diary, it is likely that pigs were kept and killed and the meat used to supply his household.

In the early years of his pastorate, the parochial house was also the home of the curate, Fr Carty.[149] The composition of the household staff is not all that clear. There was a house-keeper. Whether Fr Dungan brought or hired his own or inherited the late Fr Joy Dean's Betty cannot be established. There were frequent changes of house-keeper over the 32 years. Miss O'Halloran was hired as house-keeper in January 1857.[150] Anne Crilly was her maid.[151] There is no record of Miss O'Halloran's wages but Anne Crilly received 2s. 6d. a week at this time.[152] A later housekeeper, Catherine Martin also looked after the vestry and received 5s., three times a year, for this extra work.[153] Given the size of the parochial house (eleven rooms), the absence of all labour-saving devices and the relentless level of hospitality given by Fr Dungan, the housekeeper's life was far from easy and Anne Crilly's was even harder again.

In the diary there is a newspaper cutting entitled 'Shirt Fronts' which illustrates the labour intensive nature of housekeeping at this time.

> The glossing iron should always be heated on a closed stove or the steel surface gets dirtied or scratched. You work with it pretty much as an ordinary iron only it goes more quickly as the surface is already smooth and stiff. Iron from the point towards the neck, leaning your weight fully and evenly on the iron. If the front is of good material and well starched a perfect and brilliant gloss should be simply a question of care. For the starch dissolve a little borax in some cold water (about a teaspoonful is enough for a good basin of starch). When well mixed, stir in sufficient white starch and a little 'linen glaze' which any chemist will supply. Knead the collars and fronts thoroughly in this mixture, rubbing it well and evenly into them: clap them and ring them out; then roll them up in a clean cloth, taking care one piece does not touch the other. Leave them till you wish to iron them and if dry sprinkle with a little cold water. Iron them carefully with an ordinary iron, then damp them lightly with a clean wet muslin rag, and use the glossing iron steadily, till the proper gloss is attained; and hang them before the fire to dry.[154]

Why did Fr Dungan cut this out and place it in his diary? Was it a 'memo' to his house-keeper? Was there an implied criticism that his laundry could be better done?

Consider the domestic implications of the following entry in the diary for 9 June 1853: 'Confirmation given here by Doctors Cullen and Gillooley. Nineteen for dinner.'[155] At this stage there were two curates sharing the parochial house with Fr Dungan.[156] While these special occasions would have required much special effort to go off smoothly, they were not all that unusual. Fr Dungan welcomed friend and stranger, rich and poor and 'made hospitality his special care'. Breakfasts were provided for the church collectors,[157] Christmas parties for the vestry boys, and dinners on a weekly basis for his committee members, members of the confraternities, friends and fellow priests.[158] The parochial house was an open house where people came not only to dine but to stay for several days or weeks at a time.

There are no references to Fr Dungan's family in the diary, but one assumes that young Robert Dungan who went home on 6 August 1845 after spending some time in the parochial house was a relative.[159] Christmas 1845 was a busy time for the household staff. Mrs Walshe and her three children, also Anne Burke and Mary Dungan, all arrived on 22 December and remained until 29 December.[160] Is this the same Mary Dungan who went into St Vincent's hospital on 20 January 1855?[161] Fr Dungan brought her home to the parochial house on 12 February of the same year where she died two days later at the age of 21.[162] Fr Dungan officiated at her funeral in Glasnevin cemetery on Friday, 16 February.[163] Her month's mind Mass was celebrated in St Brigid's on 15 March followed by a dinner in the parochial house to which curates and close parish friends were invited.[164] Two years later, Mrs Anne Dungan left the parochial house after a month's severe illness.[165] She went to stay with Mrs Fagan in Pecks Lane (about a half-mile away) where she died on 20 April 1858.[166] Who was this lady? Was she his mother or his sister-in-law? Could she have come to stay with Fr Dungan after the death of Robert Dungan in Lusk in January 1856? Young Robert Dungan and his sister, Catherine spent three weeks in the parochial house after that death.[167] There is not even a hint that these were his relatives but the evidence suggests some family ties.

On 21 October 1853 the little daughter of Matt Kenna came to stay with Fr Dungan for a few weeks.[168] One wonders why the child stayed with the parish priest at this time. Was it because her father was in prison? Fr Dungan visited Matthew Kenna in the Richmond penitentiary on 6 June 1854.[169]

Fr Dungan's hospitality was especially appreciated by the founder of the Holy Ghost Congregation in Ireland.[170] Père Leman and three companions arrived in Blanchardstown on 28 October 1859.[171] They were about to establish a seminary in the building vacated by the Carmelite nuns who had moved to Hampton, Drumcondra, in 1858.[172] The French priests hired a conveyance in Dublin to transport themselves and their cargo to Blanchardstown. Having inspected their house and visited the nearby parish church to greet the Lord, they called on the parish priest and his curate, Fr John Leonard. Leman wrote to Paris the next day:[173]

> The pastor and his curate were very kind to us. When we arrived they
> pressed us to join them for tea and invited us to breakfast next
> morning. It is so embarrassing not to be able to say even one word in

conversation with these good men, or with any of the others with whom we have to deal.[174]

Fr Leman had a crash course in English in the Irish college in Paris from a clerical student from Cork.[175] Obviously this did not equip him to communicate comfortably with Fathers Dungan and Leonard.

The reception they received in Blanchardstown was in stark contrast with what happened when they visited Dr Cullen, archbishop of Dublin.[176] They had to queue for two hours and when he emerged from a conference with several bishops he did not even ask them to take a seat.[177] It was Fr Dungan's letter of introduction that helped ease their first encounter with the archbishop. Fr Dungan wrote:

> Not merely am I content, but I am full of joy to have such holy men in my parish and I do not doubt that when they learn enough English they will be of great service for the glory of God.[178]

The Holy Ghost Fathers remained in Blanchardstown for a very short time – from October 1859 to July 1860.[179] It is likely that with the proximity of St Vincent's Castleknock, the French fathers found that it was not a suitable venue for another similar educational establishment. Perhaps they had never intended to stay permanently in Blanchardstown, but had used it as a temporary abode while they looked around for more suitable accommodation. They moved to Williamstown in 1860, where they set up the French College of the Immaculate Heart of Mary, better known as Blackrock College.[180]

Fr Leman invited the Sisters of St Joseph of Cluny to take over the remaining three year lease on the building just vacated by the Holy Ghost community.[181] Once again Fr Dungan was welcoming and helpful to the French sisters.[182] When they moved to Mount Sackville four years later he kept in contact with them, acting as friend and advisor.[183] In 1864, the former convent building was leased to James Halpin, factory owner and close friend of Fr Dungan.[184] The building has continued to the present as the premises of a commercial concern.

Fr Dungan lived in an age which predated the telephone and radio. The newspaper was the only vehicle of communication available to him and he used it widely. When Edward Reilly of Ballycoolin left a bequest of £20 to the parish in 1854,[185] Fr Dungan considered it was worth 1s. 6d. to advertise this fact in the *Freeman's Journal*.[186] Subscriptions to church and school building funds were always published in the daily papers, as were the results of the various raffles, with the names of the winners and the winning ticket number.[187] Charity sermons and the sums raised were widely published. There are regular payments recorded in the parish accounts for insertions to the *Freeman's Journal* and *Morning News*.[188]

Hard-working and very active in his out-of-doors pastoral and social activities, Fr Dungan showed a similar industry and energy when he sat down at his desk to keep parish records up to date, to attend to his accounts and to record personal memoranda. Nothing was omitted, nothing left to chance. He did not depend on keeping things in his head, everything was committed to paper. He was precise and concise in everything he did. He noted the amount of interest gained on personal savings and railway shares and where they were held. He carefully recorded the deaths of individuals, fatal accidents in the parish, his attendance at funerals, weddings, religious professions, conferences, priests' retreats and tea parties.[189]

The diary is a record of a personal, parochial world. Even significant happenings in the Catholic Church in the wider world go unrecorded. There is no reference to the death of Pope Gregory XVI in 1846 or to the election of the new pope, Pius IX, or the definition of the dogma of the Immaculate Conception in 1854. There is no personal reflection nor indeed any reference to national events except when they impinge on the parish or relate directly to the parish priest. The diary is quite simply the record of the personal activities of Fr Dungan.

Politically, the diary is not very revealing. On 15 August 1843, St Brigid's Brass Band is reported to have marched to the hill of Tara for Daniel O'Connell's monster Repeal meeting.[190] It was very likely that many parishioners marched with them. Perhaps, Fr Dungan went too. He was one of the twenty-four priests of Fingal who signed the original requisition for the Repeal meeting to be held at Clontarf on Sunday, 8 October 1843.[191] This meeting was suppressed by the lord lieutenant on Saturday, 7 October.[192] Edward McDonagh of Mecklenburg Street was dispatched to Blanchardstown to carry Daniel O'Connell's warning not to travel to Clontarf. McDonagh reported that the government proclamation was not posted in the Blanchardstown and Castleknock areas.[193]

In 1848, Rome became alarmed following reports in English newspapers that Irish priests were involved in political matters.[194] Archbishop Murray was asked to urge his priests to avoid getting entangled in politics.[195] In July 1848, his archbishop conveyed these instructions to Fr Dungan.[196] From his reply, it is clear that Fr Dungan had participated in the formation of a political club, but following this directive he wrote to Archbishop Murray,

> I have endeavoured to repair any injury that my example as being present may have done, the attempted formation of any association is totally abandoned and this neighbourhood and parish will continue with God's assistance, to be what is has been remarkable for, perfectly quiet and peaceable.[197]

He concluded that he had been 'taught a lesson that would remain with him for the remainder of his life'.[198]

Three days after Fr Dungan wrote this letter, two hundred armed club men, under the leadership of Eugene O'Reilly and Thomas Clarke Luby, planned to rendezvous at Blanchardstown and, marching from there, to join up with the Navan Young Irelanders.[199] Their plans were betrayed to Dublin Castle and only sixteen men gathered in Blanchardstown. Thomas Clarke Luby later wrote that his active part in Irish revolutionary business dated from his Blanchardstown adventure. He was of the opinion that with the slightest variation of circumstances they might have changed the whole face of the national movement of 1848, in which event the Blanchardstown adventure, instead of proving as it did one abortion among many, would probably, today be spoken of as one of the boldest and most electrifying exploits in history.[200]

On 13 July 1852, a political meeting was held in St Brigid's chapel yard.[201] This was to support candidates Lentagne and Craven of the Independent Irish Party at Westminster.[202] Nine days later, Fr Dungan voted for the first time at Kilmainham,[203] presumably supporting those candidates. He seems to have taken his bishop's admonition to heart and, wherever his sympathies lay, there was no outward political expression of them as far as can be established.

Fr Dungan was blessed with practical common sense to which he brought energy, enthusiasm, perseverance and an ability to get on with people. He had the gift of being able to mobilise and motivate them to work harmoniously with him to get essential parish projects off the ground and to bring them to a satisfactory conclusion.

St Brigid's Seminary Blanchardstown under the patronage of the Most Rev. D.D. Troy and Murray, instituted in 1810; Rev. Joy Dean, President, and two residing clergymen. This seminary is designed for the education of young gentlemen. It stands in a beautiful and healthy situation, built under the immediate inspection of Rev. Mr. Dean. The halls and dormitories by air funnels introduce an abundant supply of fresh air.

English	Latin
Greek	French
Italian	German
Spanish and Portuguese languages	Writing
Arithmetic	Book-Keeping
Necessary branches of Mathematics	History

Mr. Dean concludes the studies each year with lectures on experimental philosophy. Quarterly examinations are held to which the relations of the young students are invited.

Prospectus – St Brigid's Seminary (Academy) Blanchardstown.
As advertised in the *Catholic Directory*, 1821.

2. A church in transition

When Fr Dungan arrived in Blanchardstown he inherited a very basic parochial infrastructure. This parochial poverty is well illustrated in a visitation report drawn up by Fr Joy Dean in 1831, just five years before the appointment of Fr Dungan.[1] According to that report there were in Blanchardstown chapel seven suits of old vestments, four of which were scarcely 'decent' and were not used, two suits of altar linens, three albs, some odd vestments, two old missals and one silver chalice.[2] For the two chapels-of-ease, Porterstown and Chapelizod, there was one old suit of vestments and a silver chalice.[3] He left Blanchardstown much better endowed. This expansion will form the theme of this chapter. The new church of St Brigid was in the process of construction when Fr Dungan was appointed parish priest.[4] However, it was only a shell and his first task was its completion.[5] The builders were owed £100 and there was no money in the parish fund, so fundraising had to begin.[6] He established a penny collection which enabled him to put in windows and doors, and to floor the sanctuary and part of the body of the church.[7] When the first Mass was celebrated in the new church on Sunday, 29 October 1837, the ceiling was still not in place, there were no seats, the walls were bare and there were no Stations of the Cross.[8] But a start had been made. The pride of the people and their confidence in the new parish priest ensured that from every area within the parish and from outside the parish also, right across the social spectrum, money was subscribed. Nevertheless, it took until July 1866 before all the work was completed on St Brigid's Church, Blanchardstown.[9] There is a record of the progress of the work, the names of the people involved and the costs incurred both in the diary and in the account books.

The completion of St Brigid's was only one of Fr Dungan's church building projects. As early as September 1843 he had procured the lease of a site for a new church in the Chapelizod end of the parish to replace the existing church.[10] The site for this church was leased from Viscount Palmerstown and the foundation stone laid on 8 September 1843 by Dr Yore.[11] On 14 September 1844, Fr Dungan and two Chapelizod parishioners, Mr Liddy, a paper manufacturer, and Mr Fitzpatrick, treasurer of the Confraternity of Christian Doctrine, went to Liverpool to collect for the new church in Chapelizod.[12] The three of them remained in Liverpool until 25 September and their expenses for this fund-raising expedition came to £5 each.[13] There is no record of what the Liverpool collection realised. Neither do we know how much Fr Dungan raised on the three days he spent collecting for Chapelizod church, in Dublin on 20, 21 and 22 August 1845.[14] He obviously did well, as the church was completed in record

3 Church of the Nativity of the Blessed Virgin Mary, Chapelizod.

time. It was solemnly dedicated and Mass celebrated in it by Archbishop Murray on Trinity Sunday, 3 June 1849[15] (fig. 3). The contrast between the new Church of the Blessed Virgin Mary at Chapelizod and the previous church can be seen by a comparison of their net annual valuation. The old church had a valuation of £12 while the new building had a valuation of £60.[16]

With Chapelizod church opened, attention was again focused on Blanchardstown. The only work done there in the 1843–9 period was the erection of the chapel gates, piers and wall in 1844 at a cost of £13.[17] In October 1849, the weekly penny collection resumed and in two years £130. 11s. 5d. was collected.[18] Gradually, the physical fabric of the church was improved. The flooring and altar were completed, seats were purchased and a large porch erected.[19] Two paintings were purchased and placed on each side of the main altar on 15 August 1854.[20] Fr Dungan bought the old pulpit from his former parish of Meath Street for ten shillings, on 11 March 1854.[21] He had it erected in time for the charity sermon preached by Fr H.J. Rorke SJ, on 22 July 1855.[22]

The original lease on the Blanchardstown chapel site was made by John Warren, Corduff, to the Revd Christopher Wall, parish priest of Blanchardstown, on 1 November 1785.[23] This land owned by the Warrens passed to Peter

Locke through marriage and through marriage again to Henry Darley, who renewed the lease for 999 years with Fr Dungan on 11 August 1855.[24] A deed of trust was signed between Revd Michael Dungan on the one part and John Rorke and Charles Kennedy on the other, whereby the chapel of Blanchardstown on a plot of ground containing twenty perches, was vested in them as trustees, with regulations affecting the rights of the parish priest and the appointment of trustees.[25] The ground rent was fixed at 5s. a year.[26]

On Sunday, 1 June 1856, a meeting was held in Blanchardstown chapel to raise subscriptions towards completing the ceiling, plastering and, if possible, finishing the chapel in Blanchardstown.[27] The total amount subscribed on the day was £219, given by 126 people.[28] The donations ranged from £20 given by Fr Dungan's close friend, James Reilly, £5 from Archbishop Cullen, £5 from Revd Philip Dowley, St Vincent's. Fr Dungan himself gave £5 and there were several subscriptions of 2s. 6d. and 1s.[29] Such was the enthusiasm and commitment of the parishioners that on the following Sunday, 8 June 1856, the committee agreed to proceed at once with the plastering of the chapel and the erection of the ceiling.[30] This work was carried out by Patrick Mayers of Conyngham Road, at a cost of £382 and was completed in time for the Christmas ceremonies of 1856.[31]

On Sunday, 25 January 1857, the committee held a further public meeting in the chapel.[32] The parishioners were thanked for their generosity and future plans were put before them.[33] They were told that since the 1 June meeting, the sum of £430 had been expended on the ceiling, plastering, putting up gutters and beams for the intended gallery of the Blanchardstown church.[34] The secretary of the fund-raising committee, Mr John Kelly, told the assembled parishioners, 'We now have the happiness, thank God, to behold this temple, now twenty-one years built and with every shilling paid'.[35] Again, the parishioners and those who held property, but did not reside in the parish were thanked 'for their cheerful, ready and cordial co-operation in completing the inside work of the House of God'.[36]

At this point, Mr Kelly outlined plans for the erection of a gallery, the 'want of which had been long felt', a tower entrance, according to the original design of the building, and improvement of the present sanctuary.[37] He told the parishioners that as Fr Dungan hoped to have Confirmation administered and a mission conducted in the parish in a few months, it was hoped that the principal part of the work would be completed, if possible, against that time.[38] 'This church will then be every way commodious for the people, an honour to religion and a proof of the piety and generosity of the parishioners.'[39] Once again, the parishioners responded generously and a second contract was signed with Mayers for the erection of the gallery and tower and for the opening of a side entrance. This work cost £378.[40]

Though the chapel was still not completed, it was dedicated on Sunday, 20 September 1857, by Dr Whelan, archbishop of Bombay.[41] On 18 February

1858, Beardswood and Sons were paid £308. 8s. 3d. for building the spire and portion of the tower.[42] The chapel bell, weighing 15 cwt and costing £126. 12s. 0d. was blessed by Dr Cullen on 4 January 1863.[43] The money for the bell was raised by a halfpenny a week collection commenced in August 1860.[44] The sound of the Angelus was again heard in public in the area for the first time in 300 years.[45] The Stations of the Cross were erected on 1 October 1863 at a cost of £50.[46] Once again Fr Dungan resorted to a raffle to raise the necessary funds. A silver snuff box was raffled on 16 August and raised the sum of £47.10s.[47]

Thus, the construction of St Brigid's, started in 1835 by Fr Joy Dean, was completed by Fr Dungan in 1863. The unique design of the spire is attributed to Fr Joy Dean.[48] The spire is said to be of Flemish design and Fr Joy Dean is thought to have got his inspiration from his travels on the continent.[49] The spire is one of the most distinctive features of St Brigid's and can be seen from many approaches to Blanchardstown.

In addition to the completion of St Brigid's and the building of the Church of the Nativity in Chapelizod, Fr Dungan had responsibility for the chapel of ease in Porterstown. In April 1852, a board floor was finally completed in this chapel.[50] Fr Dungan and his committee commenced a collection in Porterstown on Sunday, 31 August 1856 for building a vestry, repairing the roof, wainscoting walls and fitting a new and larger door.[51] The records show that by 1859, all the necessary repairs and improvements had been carried out in St Mochta's chapel of ease, Porterstown.[52]

It is unlikely that Fr Dungan engaged in the common practice of allowing wealthy parishioners either to erect their own pews in prominent positions in the church or to rent pews to the richer parishioners. If this had been the case, it would have been recorded in the account books. Perhaps Fr Dungan was aware of the divisions that had been created in the time of Fr Joy Dean when the young gentlemen of the academy and their masters had the sole use of the gallery in the old church.[53] Because of his frequent visits to Swords he would have been aware of the situation which had developed there in 1828 when the Taylor family, who gave land for the building of the new church, built a 'commodious servants' pew'.[54] Fr Carey, parish priest, wrote to Archbishop Murray expressing anxiety that there would be 'trouble and rioting', as the parishioners would not like to see 'the servants of the Taylors sitting up in front while they struggle in a crowd for a seat'.[55] Not alone had the Taylors erected the pews in the church but they had insured them for £110,[56] so presumably they were not overly concerned if they were damaged during these 'riots'. Fr Dungan would have avoided any arrangement which would lead to conflict or division. Everything about his dealings with people suggests his commitment to equality and harmony.

As the nineteenth century advanced, the Catholic Church was becoming more church centred due to the efforts of Bishops Troy and Murray. The Mass was the central act of worship in the church, but the counter-reformation devotions were well developed, particularly in urban areas.[57] They probably integrated existing local devotions. Blanchardstown was a typical example. One of the main methods adopted by the Catholic Church of this period to provide its laity with a knowledge of the doctrines of their religion was the preaching of the parish clergy.[58] The people of Blanchardstown were exposed to a great variety of preachers. According to Fr McNamara, Joy Dean preached regularly even towards the end of his life when his 'voice could not be heard beyond the altar rails'.[59] He also encouraged the Vincentians to preach in the three churches of the parish.[60] So convinced was he of the importance of preaching that on one particular Sunday when Fr McNamara was standing in for Joy Dean and saying the 6 a.m. Mass in Blanchardstown, the 9 a.m. in Porterstown and the 12 noon in Blanchardstown, the parish priest insisted that a sermon be preached, but conceded that if Fr McNamara 'felt too much fatigued', he need not preach at the last Mass in Blanchardstown.[61] Fr Joy Dean, in the words of Fr McNamara, was a man of special phrases, and frequently he would express himself in Latin.[62] One wonders how much of his preaching was understood and how was it received by the people of Blanchardstown. Was he, like Canon Sheehan's parish priest, intruding the classics when they wanted theology?[63]

One thing is certain. The preaching styles of Fr Joy Dean and of his successor were very different. Fr Dungan left no copies of sermons, unlike some of his successors, but one feels sure that his style of preaching was characteristically simple, direct and in tune with the needs of his people. Perhaps, he used materials like the *Sixteen sermons in an easy and familiar style*, published in 1736 by Bishop James Gallagher of Raphoe.[64] One wonders if some of the newspaper cuttings found in the diary were used as homiletic resources, for example, a cutting entitled 'Regularity of habit' offers practical advice and also sums up Fr Dungan himself:[65]

> One of the most difficult of all the minor habits to acquire is that of regularity. It ranks with that of order. The natural inclination of most persons is to defer until the last possible moment, or to put off to another time, where this can possibly be done. Yet habits of regularity contribute largely to the ease and comfort of life. A person can multiply his efficiency by it. We know persons who have a multitude of duties, and who perform a vast deal of work daily, who set apart certain hours for given duties, and are there at the moment and attend rigidly to what is in hand. This done, and other engagements are met, each in order, and a vast deal accomplished, not by strained exertion but by regularity. The mind can be so trained to this that at certain hours in the day it will turn to a particular line of duty, and at other hours to other and different labours. The very diversity is restful, when attended to in regular order. But let these be run together, and the duties mixed, and

what before was easy is now annoying and oppressive. And the exact difference between many is just at this point. There are those who confuse and rush, and attempt to do several things at once and accomplish little, while another will quietly proceed from one duty to another, and easily accomplish a vast amount of work. The difference is not in the capacity of the two, but in the regular methods of the one, as compared with the irregular and confused habits of the other.

How did the women of Blanchardstown and indeed the men respond to his homily on the 'Cheerful wife'?

The magnetism of her smile, the electrical brightness of her looks and movements infect every eye. The children go to school with the sense of something great to be achieved; the husband goes out to the world in a conqueror's spirit. No matter how people annoy and worry him through the day, far off her presence shines and he whispers to himself, 'At home I shall find rest.' So day by day she literally renews his strength and energy. And, if you know a man with a beaming face, a kind heart and a prosperous business, in nine cases out of ten you will find he has a wife of this kind.[66]

His reflections on the importance of good habits and on the cheerful wife may not have been used in the way suggested but those pieces were important enough to him to be kept in his diary.

On 3 July 1849 all the parish priests of the Dublin diocese received a circular letter from Dean Hamilton asking the clergy and the people if they believed in the doctrine of the Immaculate Conception and if they thought that the pope should define it as an article of faith.[67] The reply had to be sent to Archbishop Murray before 24 July.[68] Fr Dungan replied on 23 July.[69] Obviously he had preached on this subject on the intervening Sundays. He was able to assure the archbishop that the people of Blanchardstown 'all believe the doctrine and hope it will be defined'.[70] He also stated that the Office of the Immaculate Conception was recited regularly by the members of the Confraternity of Christian Doctrine.[71] It is clear that he did elicit the views of his parishioners. How he did this cannot be determined. In contrast, Fr Carey of Swords had sent back his reply by 18 July.[72] He told the archbishop that the people of Swords were silent on the subject and 'silence gave consent'.[73]

Fr Dungan was very involved in developing the devotional life of his parishioners by the formation of sodalities and confraternities and by the provision of programmes of catechesis and evangelisation.[74] Religious instruction of the young was partly catered for by the schools, but since the majority of children did not attend school on a regular basis, their needs were generally met by the establishment of special catechism classes in the parish chapel.[75] In Blanchardstown, lay participation was organised on a systematic basis through the establishment of Confraternities of Christian Doctrine.[76]

The Confraternity of Christian Doctrine had its origins in sixteenth-century Italy.[77] When exactly it was introduced into Ireland is impossible to determine. There is proof that it was well established in Ireland by 1824 from the *First Report of Commissioners on Education in Ireland*:

> In the year 1800, a society was established for the purpose of giving instruction in the principles of the Roman Catholic faith and Christian piety. It is composed of laymen and is called the Sodality of Christian Doctrine. It is, in fact a society of catechists. The duty of the members is to attend every Sunday in the chapel and instruct the children in the Catechism. Certain indulgences were granted by Pope Pius for the encouragement of the members of this society. Sodalities, or as they were frequently termed, confraternities, of this character are established in many of the towns and most populous parishes of the south and west of Ireland, and appear to be daily extending themselves to other parts of the country. Each confraternity has its own particular rules and regulations approved by the Roman Catholic bishop of the diocese. The members are obliged to receive Holy Communion monthly, to exercise vigilant superintendence over the moral conduct of each other, and to devote themselves on Sundays, in the chapel, to the catechetical instruction of the Roman Catholic children. A lending library of religious books is usually attached to each of these confraternities.

When Archbishop Murray visited St Brigid's, Blanchardstown for Confirmation in June 1839, Fr Dungan reported that catechism was taught every Sunday, before and after Mass in the three chapels, by the schoolteachers with a few assistants.[78]

At that time, he reported that there was no formal Confraternity of the Christian Doctrine in the parish.[79] However, it was well established and was flourishing by 1844.[80] It was highly organised with a male and a female branch and a Purgatorian Society, all with clearly set out duties and obligations under the supervision of Fr Dungan and Fr Burke CM of St Vincent's, Castleknock.[81]

There are twelve rules of the confraternity set out in the Confraternity Book.[82] One assumes that these are the general rules for the conduct of the confraternity, not just in Blanchardstown, but in the archdiocese of Dublin. The rules embody much of what is written in the 1824 *Report* already mentioned regarding the catechetical nature of the confraternity and the role within it of the local clergy. The following is written under Rules of the Confraternity for Blanchardstown.

> They that instruct many into justice
> shall shine as stars for all eternity (Daniel, 21: 3).

The rules follow. For admission to this confraternity it was required that members be enrolled in a book kept for that purpose by the president, 'for the formation, improvement and preservation of this society and that its labours may be efficient'.[83]

There were 26 male members listed for September 1846.[84] It was noted that one person, Thomas Lacey had left the parish, Joseph Strong had resigned, and Patrick English had ceased to be a member.[85] In 1847, there were 21 members in the female confraternity.[86] They followed the same rules but paid an entrance of 6*d.* instead of the 1*s.* 2*d.* entrance for men.[87] That all the rules of the confraternity were strictly adhered to is evident from the minutes of the election of new members. An example will illustrate. On Sunday, 9 November 1845, at a general meeting at which the Revd Mr Dungan presided, Patrick Fitzpatrick, after serving two months probation was unanimously elected. The minutes were signed by J. Quinn, president, L. Bourke, secretary and Fr Burke, St Vincent's Castleknock.[88] It is clear from the minutes that the male and female sections operated separately. For example the minutes for 7 December 1845 note that:

> At a general meeting held on this day at which the Revd Mr Dungan presided, Alice Cassidy was unanimously elected having served two months probation. Proposed by Bridget Callaghan and seconded by Bridget Roe. Fanny Moran commenced two months probation.[89]

In accordance with the general rules, elections of officers were to be held on the first Sunday of January each year. The minutes of the election held on Sunday, 4 January 1846 are recorded in the Confraternity Book:

> On Sunday January 4th at a general meeting held on this day at which the Revd Mr Burke (St Vincent's Castleknock) presided, the annual election took place, returning as president John Quinn, vice president James Kennedy, treasurer Peter Fitzsimons. The secretary was not named in Mr Dungan's absence.[90]

The male and female elections appear to have been conducted at the same meeting:- 'Female confraternity elected president Catherine Kearns, vice president Bridget Callaghan.'[91] It is clear from the account books that the penalties for non attendance or failure to receive Holy Communion each month, were strictly enforced. For the year 1847, February to November, there are five fines recorded ranging from 6*d.* to 2*d.*[92] – the precise nature of the 'offence' is not stated.

The confraternity fulfilled a two-fold purpose: the personal formation and sanctification of the members and the instruction of the children of the parish. Undoubtedly, it fulfilled a deep social need also for people to come together. There was a certain status attached to membership. On 12 October 1845, at a general meeting held in the chapel in Blanchardstown in which the Fr Dungan presided, it was agreed to by the members of the confraternity without dissent that the monthly appearance of members in surplices shall in future be strictly carried out.[93] It was decided at the commencement of Lent 1846 that the members should meet in the chapel on Sunday, Wednesday, and Friday during Lent and recite the Rosary of the Blessed Virgin.[94] Typical of the devotional aspect of the confraternity is the following entry:

> In Blanchardstown chapel on Good Friday, 1846, the members assembled and performed the evening devotions, by the Rosary of the Blessed Virgin and the Litany of Saints, with a chapter of a pious work, read by the vice president.[95]

Another aspect of the work of the confraternity is seen in an entry for Sunday, 22 March 1846:

> On this day the number of boys and girls under the instruction of the members of the Confraternity of the Christian Doctrine received the Temperance Pledge from Rev Mr Burke of St Vincent's College in addition to which a great number [boys and girls] on St Patrick's Day also took the pledge.
>
> Under the special sanction of Rev Mr Burke, they previously received notice to consult with their parents in full and sufficient time, the result of which and the free consent of themselves leaves it to be recorded as one of the things well worthy of a place in our minutes, and a circumstance which with infinite pleasure I take this liberty to insert with the fullest confidence in the future and permanent benefit of the children, with no small degree of satisfaction to all in our confraternity.[96]

Signed: L. Bourke, President
            James Kennedy, Vice President
            22 March 1846

Membership of the Christian Doctrine Confraternity averaged between 40 to 60 in its first 10 years in the parish.[97] Enthusiasm seems to have waned in the late 1850s. At an extraordinary meeting of the confraternity in August 1859, it was resolved that 'each member should do their utmost endeavour to augment the society by inducing others to join'.[98] The drive for new membership was not successful. It is noted that no meeting was held on 12 February 1871 and at the 12 March meeting, there were only seven males and 11 females present.[99]

Despite the decline in membership of the confraternity, the catechism classes continued to be an important part of the religious education of children. On some Sundays in 1856 there were up to 300 children present.[100] In 1871, the average attendance each Sunday morning was 138 children.[101] The children were divided into four or five classes and supplied with catechisms by the members of the confraternity. There was an elaborate system of premiums for rewarding the children:

> Every boy or girl who attends at catechism and is not five minutes late is entitled to a white ticket.
>
> Every boy and girl who is present before prayer commences, who is well conducted and who misses less than three questions in the day's lesson, appointed on preceding Sunday is entitled to a blue ticket – a blue ticket is to be equal in value to two white ones.
>
> Every boy and girl who succeeds in getting twelve white tickets or six blue ones, is entitled to a yellow ticket. No child to be entitled to a blue ticket who is *either late for Mass*, or disorderly in the church.
>
> Premiums to be given to every child who holds three yellow tickets at the end of each year. The premium to vary in value in accordance with the number of tickets held by each child. No child to be entitled to any premium who holds less than three white or three yellow at the end of the year.
>
> No child to be entitled to a blue ticket who is not learning the 2nd or 3rd size catechism.[102]

> Signed M. Dungan P.P., Sunday, 8 Oct. 1865.

In the Confraternity Account Book, it is noted that 9½d. was received from children for catechisms in December 1845[103] and 7s. 2d. for catechisms in February 1846.[104] Fr Dungan paid 14s. 6d. for catechisms on 14 January 1846[105] and a payment for forty class books is recorded on 15 February 1846.[106] This is a typical account. The first catechism cost one halfpenny.[107]

The rules of the Confraternity stated that the children be divided into different classes according to the following order:

> 1st class, prayers including the Acts of Faith, Hope and Charity
> 2nd class, small catechisms
> 3rd class, abridgement of the general catechism
> 4th class, general catechism
> 5th class, Fleury's Historical Catechism. But to this last one, no one is to be admitted but such as shall be declared fit by some priest of the chapel.[108]

The Christian Doctrine Confraternity incorporated a Purgatorian Society. The aims of this society were to administer comfort to dying persons, to relieve suffering souls in Purgatory and to extirpate drunkenness at wakes.[109] For a long time the Catholic clergy had condemned the practices prevalent at wakes which they regarded as occasions of excessive drinking and temptations to sexual immorality. Statutes for the diocese of Dublin introduced in 1831 attempted to curb such excesses. 'Drunken vigils for the dead were forbidden, they were to be gradually abolished and those who favoured them rebuked.'[110] In 1832, there was a major outbreak of cholera in Dublin. The first case reported in the parish was on 23 April 1832.[111] By 1833, there were 119 cases of cholera in the area.[112] Archbishop Murray sent a pastoral letter to the clergy and people of the diocese on 25 April 1832 warning them that 'the practice of waking the dead is most dangerous to public health, during the continuance of this destructive malady'.[113] It is against this background that the aims and activities of the Purgatorian Society must be seen. There are references to this society in the parish from 1845 onwards.[114] The special rules are written in the confraternity book.[115] The duties of the Purgatorian Society give a very interesting insight into the practices prevalent at wakes in the parish at this time which will be discussed later in the chapter.

It is very likely that the members of the confraternity were also enrolled in the Confraternity of the Sacred Heart. On 21 November 1828, Dr Murray granted by authority from Rome, to the Church of St Brigid, Blanchardstown, all the privileges conceded to this confraternity.[116] In 1830, Fr Joy Dean recorded that there were twenty-four enrolled in the Confraternity of the Sacred Heart.[117] There is a very strong tradition in Fr Joy Dean's family that he was very devoted to the Sacred Heart and was one of those who popularised this devotion in Ireland.[118] He translated from the French and revised a prayer book entitled *Devotion to the Sacred Heart*.[119] No copy of this book survives in the parish archive, but according to his great great nephew Fr Philip Deane, Multyfarnham, a member of the family in Carrickfergus still has a copy.[120]

That there was an increase in church-centred devotions in Blanchardstown is clearly reflected in the parish records. Between 1825 and 1830, Fr Joy Dean enrolled 119 parishioners in the scapular.[121] On Tuesday, 13 August, Fr Dungan received the privilege of giving the Scapular of Our Lady of Mount Carmel – from Fr O'Brien, Superior of Clarendon Street Friary.[122] In his diary, there is a section devoted to naming the persons he invested with this scapular – the 'brown' scapular – for each year from August 1850 to June 1858 – date and month being given when each person was invested as well as the address.[123] For example, 28 persons – both male and female – were invested in 1851.[124] There are also lists of persons enrolled in the red scapular for 1852, 1853, 1854 and 1857.[125]

There was an active Society of St Vincent de Paul in the parish.[126] There are entries for collections for Christmas charities. For example in 1867 Fr J.

Leonard after giving details, states that this account was transferred into the account of the Society of St Vincent de Paul, Blanchardstown (£8. 9s. 8½d.) as well as all sums that came in afterwards.[127]

During Fr Dungan's pastorate there are many references to novenas in the parish. An entry in his diary for 6 August 1855 states that he commenced a novena for the Assumption in the Blanchardstown chapel.[128] The feast of the patroness of the parish, St Brigid, was celebrated in a very special way each year. On 1 February 1862, Fr Dungan celebrated High Mass with sermon and Benediction, 'it being the patroness-day'.[129] Again in 1865, it is recorded that there was High Mass, Benediction, a special sermon preached by Fr Burke of St Vincent's, and a collection made for St Vincent de Paul Society on St Brigid's Day, 1 February.[130] Fr Dungan was quite ill at this time and had not celebrated Mass since 16 January.[131] In fact, he had the doctor visit him the day before the Mass.[132] Dr O'Ferrall prescribed that Fr Dungan should bathe his swollen limbs twice a day.[133] Despite all of this, he managed to be on the altar to celebrate St Brigid's feast day with his parishioners.[134] Benediction regularly took place.[135] There are many references in the account books to the buying of incense (2s. 6d.) and charcoal (3d.) and different types of candles.[136] For the year 1857 alone:

March 27	Bought at Rathbornes 6 lbs and 3 lbs of wax	19s. 6d.
June 12	Paid at Rathbornes for 6 lbs of wax at 2s. 2d. per lb	13s. 0d.
Aug. 8	6 lbs of wax	13s. 0d.
Sept. 5	6 lbs of wax	13s. 0d.
	1 lb of tapers	1s. 8d.
Sept. 19	6 lbs of wax candles	13s. 0d.
Nov. 6	6 lbs of wax candles	13s. 0d.
Nov. 30	18 lbs of altar candles	12s. 0d.[137]

Forty Hours Adoration was also a regular feature of religious life in the parish in Fr Dungan's time.[138] The expenses incurred in the advertising and conducting of this devotion are also recorded in the diary. For June 1860, the expenses were £9.1s. 0d. made up of various items.[139] There was a very active Altar Society in the parish. There is an entry in the parish account book of £21. 5s. 5d. received at a public meeting of the Altar Society held on 28 March 1858.[140]

Fr Dungan recorded in his diary that on 1 October 1863, the Stations of the Cross were erected and blessed in Blanchardstown chapel.[141] An entry for 11 November 1866 noted that the Stations of the Cross were erected and blessed in Porterstown chapel.[142] It is very likely that the erection of the Stations would have coincided with devotions to the Way of the Cross and to the Passion. The many references to the Living Rosary indicate that Fr Dungan promoted this devotion in the parish and the account books show the expenses involved in this promotion which were ongoing as well as the collections which were taken up from the members. For example 28 March 1858, per Living Rosary £5. 3s. 6d.[143] For the year 1858, the total collections from the Living Rosary amounted to £12. 7s. 6d.[144] The parish library was another initiative of Fr Dungan.[145] In 1839, there were up to 300 pious and religious books available to be given out on loan to families in the parish.[146] Some of the titles included Manning's *Short way* and the *Expositions of Bossuet*.[147]

It was not until the 1840s that the regular practice of giving parish missions got under way in Ireland.[148] Blanchardstown had the Vincentians in the parish since 1835.[149] In that year, they gave their first mission in Chapelizod.[150] The parish mission was a regular feature during Fr Dungan's pastorate.[151] There are no details regarding the early missions in the parish extant, but an altar book for 1883 indicates that, during the annual retreat in May, 1883, first Mass was celebrated at 5 a.m., second Mass at 8 a.m. On Saturday, first Mass was at 4.30 a.m.[152]

The provision of music at Mass was another innovation introduced by Fr Dungan. On the first Sunday of June 1862, a choir commenced with the harmonium in Blanchardstown chapel at second Mass.[153] Mr Lynch played the harmonium but the members of the choir were all women whose names Fr Dungan listed on the inside cover of his account book.[154] They were: Mary Jane Corcoran, Julia Delany, Mary Donnely, Anna Mooney, Eliza Mooney, Margaret Sheridan and Bridget Sullivan.[155] There were regular entries in the account book for the tuning of the harmonium and two references to repair of same: 28 September 1865, open repairs to the harmonium cost 7s. 6d. A further repair carried out on 6 December 1865 amounted to 10s.[156]

Blanchardstown was one of three parishes in Dublin which had a Temperance Society even before the arrival of Fr Theobald Mathew in Dublin in 1840.[157] According to Fr Myles Ronan, the three parishes of Blanchardstown, Palmerstown and Sandyford had already enrolled up to 30,000 before the Fr Mathew campaign began.[158] In 1841, the temperance societies in and around Dublin decided to hold a major rally and procession on St Patrick's Day in the Fifteen Acres in the Phoenix Park.[159] As part of the preparation, Fr Dungan and the Blanchardstown Temperance Society held a tea and coffee entertainment in the old chapel which 'was splendidly decorated with laurel wreaths, and transparencies with appropriate devices and there the gentry of the neighbourhood seconded their pious pastor in his exertions'.[160] Bands were attached to practically all the local temperance societies, and St Brigid's Brass Band, formed in 1826, led the Blanchardstown contingent to the great St Patrick's Day rally in the Phoenix Park, where an estimated quarter of a million people gathered.[161] There are many references in the account books to the collections taken up at the temperance society meetings. There was a personal connection between Blanchardstown parish and Fr Mathew. Fr Dungan invited him to preach the charity sermon in Chapelizod on Whit-Sunday, 31 May 1846, and upwards of £80 was collected on the day.[162]

From the account books, it is obvious that the church and everything to do with the ritual was very meticulously maintained. A recurring item in the accounts is the payment to the bell-ringer: 2s. for Sunday and 3s. for the Angelus daily per week.[163] An entry for 5 August 1849 states: Blanchardstown tabernacle being newly gilt was on the altar today and a tabernacle which cost £12 was on the same day on Porterstown altar'.[164] An interesting entry in the diary is his recording the fact that on Sunday, 6 November 1853, he commenced to wear the 'collar'.[165] On 19 August 1859, there are accounts which point to the embellishment of the altar and the elaboration of the ritual:

	£	s.	d.
High Mass vestments	40.	0.	0
3 worked linen albs	6.	0.	0
Gold antependium	4.	0.	0
Veil for tabernacle and chalice	1.	12.	0
Covering canopy	1.	14.	0
Lace hangings	2.	0.	0
Reredos of Virgin's Altar		9.	0
Stole		10.	0
12 tassels		12.	0
24 yds of calico @ 6½d.		13.	0
Flowers		10.	0
6 finger towels		9.	0
2 Corporals		3.	0
2 Purifiers		2.	0
3 Cinctures		12.	0
White Cope	5.	0.	0
Tissue paper for vestments		3.	3
Credence table		12.	0[166]

On 11 December 1860, a silver ciborium and chalice were bought for £12 and a tablecloth for the vestry for 7s. 6d.[167] On 9 March 1861, they paid 3d. for 1,000 tacks for carpets and on 19 December, they paid £1 for 12 stone china candlesticks.[168] It is all a far cry from the pitiful inventory supplied to the archbishop by Fr Dungan's predecessor, Fr Joy Dean, in 1830.[169] The newly-found confidence of the Catholic people, both clerical and lay, is demonstrated very practically in all the details of church life documented so clearly in these parish archives.

The curates had a very active involvement with the running of the parish under Fr Dungan. Fr Laurence Carty had been in the parish from at least 1832.[170] From all the records, they seemed to work very closely together and towards the end of 1849, Fr Carty took charge of the Chapelizod section of the parish.[171] He outlived Fr Dungan and remained in the parish until 1872.[172] There was nearly always a second curate: John Gallagher 1836–40; James Leahy 1850; James O'Reilly 1851–3; John O'Reilly 1854–6 and John Leonard 1857–72 who was there when Fr Dungan died.[173] This last-mentioned curate, Fr John Leonard kept very meticulous accounts. However, he had a very idiosyncratic hand and it is very difficult to decipher his handwriting. One can learn much from a study of the 'official' church and the manner in which it organised itself. However, beyond the world of the pulpit and the pew there was another world.[174] Side by side with church-centred liturgy and devotion, there co-existed the practices of popular religion. There were clearly problems associated with moving from a multi-faceted indigenous religious culture such as had existed in Ireland, to a set of rules as delineated in the decrees of Trent.[175] James Kelly suggests that Christianity and superstition were woven together in a 'powerful fusion' towards the end of the seventeenth century.[176] There is evidence of this 'fusion' continuing right into mid nineteenth-century Blanchardstown. All the evidence reflects the religious enthusiasm of the people; yet many of the Irish bishops were concerned at its heterodox expression.[177] A source of perennial anxiety was the popular celebration of festivals and patterns often connected with holy wells, since the religious observances were generally a prelude to more secular celebrations.[178] Gatherings at those holy places and the shared attendant rituals served as powerful bonding forces within local confessional communities.[179] Again, Blanchardstown was pretty typical. In Blanchardstown, people took notice of what their clergy had to say to them, but 'they also modified those ortho-doxies to reflect their own experiences, traditions and local circumstances'.[180]

The pattern was an important feature of the social and religious life of Blanchardstown. Six wells have been identified in the nineteenth-century parish: Lady's Well, Mulhuddart; Caveen Well, (St Kevin) Abbotstown; St Brigid's Well, Castleknock; the Rag Well, Diswellstown; the Rag Well, Darby's Hill, Blanchardstown; and St Mochta's Well, Clonsilla.[181] While these wells were frequented for their curative qualities, their predominant ethos was Christian.[182] The religious rites performed at the patterns held at these venues routinely involved extensive prayer.[183]

The most celebrated holy well in the parish which still survives was located in the townland of Tyrellstown, on the left hand side of the road as one approaches Mulhuddart cemetery from Blanchardstown. The well is covered by a masonry structure which is nine feet long, six feet wide and six feet high, with an opening at each end.[184] On the roof are two finials, one with a stone carved with a cross in relief and the other a stone with a niche containing a small statue of Our Lady.[185] The well is substantially the same as when Austin Cooper described it 21 October 1741.[186] The Ordnance Survey Name Books give the complete inscription as it read in 1837: 'O Blessed Mother and ever Virgin Glorious Queen of the World, make intercession for us to Our Lord, Amen.'[187] There is no tradition as to the origins of this well. Myles Ronan believed that it was possibly dedicated originally to St Cuthbert.[188] It was then re-dedicated to the Blessed Virgin when the church at Mulhuddart was erected *c.*1300.[189] It was believed that the water from this well cured sprains, cuts, bruises and rheumatism.[190] It was customary to leave small religious objects and flowers as offerings.[191] Like most holy wells, there are a number of legends associated with it. One of the local legends recounts how a group of men filled in the well, but immediately they had finished the work, the well sprang up again at the opposite side of the road.[192] While the well was visited throughout the year, there were days of special devotion. These were the major feasts dedicated to the Blessed Virgin, 25 March, 15 August, 8 September and 8 December.[193] Isaac Butler described this well in an account of a journey from Dublin to the shores of Lough Derg written *c.*1741.[194]

> About midway ascending to ye church [Mulhuddart] is an excellent well: it is carefully walled, and several large trees about it. Here on the 8 September, a great patron is kept with a vast concourse of all sexes and ages from many miles, upwards of eighty tents are pitched here furnished with all kinds of liquors and provisions for ye reception and refreshment of ye company.[195]

Here we see the social side of the pattern. The sacred and the secular had a very thin divide. It is clear that fighting and drunkenness were not unusual. In October 1760, the *Dublin Gazette* reported on an inquest held after the death of Edward Campbell, a gentleman's servant who died of wounds he received in a fray at Lady's Well.[196]

Due to the secular celebrations which accompanied the pattern, the local clergy actively discouraged the holding of it. The following notice was printed in Faulkner's *Dublin Journal* 15 August 1754:

> We are assured that the Roman Catholic clergy to prevent as far as in them lieth, the enormities and scandalous excesses that are annually committed at the well near Mulahedard, commonly called Lady's Well, have prevailed on the landowners contiguous thereto, not to permit any tents or booths to be erected hereafter on any part of their lands: of which it is judged proper to give to notice in this public manner, to prevent a disappointment to such publicans as usually erected tents or booths near said well.[197]

Despite such directives, the pattern continued into Fr Dungan's pastorate. In 1837, Samuel Lewis reported that the well was 'frequented at certain periods by the peasantry'.[198] Contemporary observers were in general very critical of these pattern day gatherings. It is not surprising that there is not one reference to them in Fr Dungan's diary. He simply offered an alternative by providing novenas in the church for major feast-days like 25 March and 15 August, the most popular pattern days at Lady's Well.[199]

The Catholic clergy had for long condemned the practices prevalent at wakes, practices which in many cases seem to have had a pre-Christian origin. The archives of the Irish Folklore Commission list some of the games that were played at wakes in the Blanchardstown area, including 'The grass that grew crooked around the crooked crab tree', 'Band master', 'Birdlost', 'Chew, chew the button', 'My man Jack', 'All hampers on the block', and 'Little bit of fish'.[200] While most of the games were harmless and were designed to help keep the people at the wake house from falling asleep, wakes were regarded by the church authorities as occasions of excessive drinking and temptations to sexual immorality.[201] Despite the warnings from the clergy, wakes continued as part of popular religion. The Purgatorian Societies were part of a sustained attempt by the church to change the nature of wakes. This is evident from a reading of the Blanchardstown society rules, particularly rules 7 to 11:

7. When a death occurs in the neighbourhood the friends will give notice to the President, or some other person appointed for the purpose, who will serve notice upon the members, either by word of mouth, or by printed tickets, to assemble in the chapel at a fixed hour, in order to proceed from thence to the wake house, to recite the Office of the Dead.

   N.B. Sometimes the schoolmaster will be found to be the most convenient person to do this, as he can readily serve the notices upon the several members by means of the children returning home from school to the several localities.

8. At the appointed hour the members will meet in the vestry, or at the chapel, and from thence proceed in edifying order to the wake house. Being arrived there they shall at once proceed to recite the Office of the Dead in solemn form. It is strictly forbidden to take anything in the way of refreshment, or accept any remuneration at the house.

9. The President, may, if he judge it expedient, remind prudently the people of the house, that those plays and games usual at wakes are strictly prohibited, and that all young persons, not members of the family are commanded, by the statutes of the archbishop to return home after night fall.

10. Should any of the members of the female confraternity wish to visit the wake house, they are to do so during the day, when they should kneel down, and recite the Rosary of Jesus, or of the Blessed Virgin Mary, with the proper litanies; but it is strictly forbidden the young women to go to the wake after night fall.

11. The President of the office will keep a list of all the deceased members of the confraternity and likewise of such persons as are recommended to their prayers, to be prayed for on Monday evenings in the weekly Office for the Dead.[202]

This chapter has examined the building and renovation of the three churches in the parish. It has outlined the programmes of evangelization and catechesis through which Fr Dungan sought to draw the community into the life of the church, and shows how the ritual, liturgy and devotional life became more elaborate and church-centred. It attempts to show the stratagems which the clergy and especially Fr Dungan employed to wean the community away from the more superstitious practices of folk-religion associated with the holy wells, the patterns and the wakes to a more orthodox observance. Fr Dungan sought to give his people 'the experience of the Mass envisioned by the decrees of Trent, which saw the ritual of the Mass as a parochial celebration led by the parish priest in an environment of splendour appropriate to the sacrament'.[203] By the end of his pastorate, the Church was held in high esteem in Blanchardstown. With the erection of chapels, through sodalities and confraternities, the people gained a sense of their dignity as Catholics, were better educated in the faith, and as a result the Church in Blanchardstown gained a status and a vitality that carried into subsequent pastorates. The parish had come a long way from the poverty portrayed in the 1831 Visitation report.[204]

3. The provision of education in the parish of Blanchardstown

The state of Irish society has changed so rapidly within the last thirty or forty years, that scarcely anyone could believe it possible for the present generation to be looked upon in many things as the descendants of that which has immediately gone before them.[1]

When William Carleton made this statement in 1840, Fr Dungan was 41 years old, four years established as parish priest of Blanchardstown, facing all the challenges and demands that went with the changing times of this ministry. The provision of educational facilities within the parish was to occupy much of Fr Dungan's time and energy over the 32 years of his pastorate. Being a man of perspicacity, he was well aware that education was the great catalyst for 'improvement'.

The national system of education had been in operation in Ireland since 1831.[2] The initial reaction of Catholics to the national system was, in general, one of quiet approval.[3] Although they did not regard it as perfect they appreciated the fact that it respected their religion and provided an opportunity for their children to be instructed in its truths.[4] Fears regarding proselytism were allayed by the presence of Archbishop Daniel Murray as one of the two Catholics on the seven commissioner board.[5] Among the voices raised in opposition to the national system of education, the loudest was that of John MacHale, the coadjutor bishop of Killala. He saw the system as a reluctant concession made as a result of pressure exerted at the general election of 1831.[6] According to MacHale, it was 'narrow, bigoted and insulting' with only one redeeming feature, and that the negative one of having incurred the opposition of the violent anti-Catholic elements in Ireland.[7]

MacHale's opinion of the national system did not mirror the general feeling among Catholics in the early 1830s.[8] Once again Blanchardstown was typical of the majority which accepted Dr Doyle's exhortation to join the system which, though not perfect, was well suited to the particular circumstances of Ireland.[9] It is against this background that education must be studied in Blanchardstown in the period 1836–68, but to put educational development in Blanchardstown parish in its historical context, it is helpful to review the events of the preceding decade.

The *Catholic Directory of 1821* and the *Second report of the Commissioners of Irish Education inquiry 1826*, give a picture of the state of Catholic education in the parish prior to the introduction of the national system of education in 1831. At that time, there were six Catholic elementary pay schools in the parish.[10] Blanchardstown school was located beside the chapel and had been established in 1762.[11] Chapelizod school was opened in 1808.[12] Mulhuddart and Lower Road schools were established in 1822.[13] There was a pay school on Blackhorse Avenue and another beside the old chapel in Porterstown.[14] There were two convent schools in the parish. The Carmelites opened a school in Blanchardstown in 1828 and had nearly 200 girls on the roll.[15] This school was in the building formerly occupied by St Brigid's Academy.[16] The Dominican nuns had a school in Cabra since 1812.[17] All of these schools were under the superintendence of the 'Roman Catholic priests and the members of the Blanchardstown Committee'.[18] The schools were financed by local subscriptions and the money received from the annual charity sermon.[19] The pupils, if they could afford it, paid 1*d.* per week to the teacher.[20]

Two of the schools were built by local landowners. Andrew Rorke of Tyrellstown, built Mulhuddart school.[21] Porterstown school, for the education of Catholic children, was located beside Porterstown chapel. It was built, endowed and supported by Luke White of Luttrellstown Castle, who placed it under the management of Fr McPharlan and who presented it to Fr Dean just before White's death in 1824.[22] However, the lease was not drawn up at the time of Luke White's death and his son, Colonel Thomas White repossessed the school and placed it under the Kildare Place Society.[23]

The 1821 *Catholic Directory* gave the following description of St Brigid's Academy/Seminary, Blanchardstown. It was under the patronage of the archbishop, Dr Troy, and instituted in 1810. Fr Joseph Joy Dean was president and there were two residing clergymen. This seminary was designed for the education of young gentlemen. According to the prospectus:

> It stands on a beautiful and healthy situation, built under the immediate inspection of Revd Mr Dean. The halls and dormitories by air funnels introduce an abundant supply of fresh air. The plan of education comprises English, Latin, Greek, French, Italian, German, Spanish and Portuguese languages; writing, arithmetic, book-keeping, history and necessary branches of mathematics. Mr Dean concludes the studies each year with lectures on experimental philosophy. Quarterly examinations are held, at which the relations of the young students are invited. The parish chapel immediately adjoins the establishment, and a gallery from the enclosure is for the sole use of these young gentlemen and masters to assist at religious duties, and to receive exhortations addressed to the congregation. During recreation the masters attend to prevent disorder and to enforce gentlemanly deportment. The age of admission is from seven to fourteen years. There are at present sixty students in the seminary.[24]

Down the road in Cabra, the Dominican nuns were running a similar type of boarding school 'where young ladies are taught the usual branches of English education, Italian, French, music, needlework, plain and ornamental'.[25] The fee in Cabra was £25 per year for pupils under 12 years and £30 for those above that age.[26] Dancing cost an extra £2 per season; washing £2 per annum.[27] The school year was long by modern standards. There was a vacation from 10 July to 10 August and the nuns were adamant that 'it will not be permitted, under any circumstances to remove a child from the school at any other season of the year'.[28] The prospectus went on to state that

> The nuns, solely intent on being usefully employed in promoting the temporal and eternal welfare of their pupils, will not in any manner sanction the imprudence of parents, who, attaching undue importance to what is called a fashionable education, waste time and money in having their children taught, to the exclusion of useful and necessary knowledge, accomplishments for which they have neither taste, capacity, nor use.
>
> No fashion is recognised in this establishment but such as becomes the children in their respective stations in life; at the same time no effort shall be left untried to make them so acquainted with the nature and fitness of things, that should circumstances permit them, fairly to rise in society, they will naturally take their own places, and fill them with propriety, ease, and dignity.
>
> This, it is respectfully submitted, is a more judicious plan for educating females, than any mode of instruction that might have a tendency to make them restless and unhappy in their proper sphere, or prematurely urge them to change their positions in society, at the risk of incurring ruinous expense, and involving themselves and their families in endless miseries.[29]

A number of Catholic children attended Church of Ireland schools in the parish. In 1826, 18 of the 26 children attending the Church of Ireland parish school in Castleknock were Catholic.[30] Thomas Ellis of Abbotstown built a school in Abbotstown demesne for the instruction of females in 'reading, writing, arithmetic and needlework'.[31] In 1826, 11 of the 16 girls attending this school were Catholic.[32] This school was associated with the Kildare Place Society and there were allegations of proselytism which led to controversy between Fr Joy-Dean and Mr Ellis. In a letter to Archbishop Murray, 26 August 1825, Ellis claimed that Fr Dean had objected to the Abbotstown school and his curate had threatened to refuse the sacraments to the teacher.[33] Ellis felt that Fr Dean 'was influenced by a conscientious, but unfounded apprehension of proselytism'.[34] Ellis also stated that Fr McPharlan, Dean's predecessor, had no such problems with the Abbotstown school. Ellis was 'anxious to employ a Catholic teacher to allay any suspicion of sinister or unworthy motive' but if Dean's opposition continued, he threatened to employ a Protestant teacher.[35] Ellis stated in another letter to Archbishop Murray that Catholic children got Saturdays free so that they could receive religious education and he invited Murray to visit the school.[36] In a further and final letter to the archbishop, Ellis expressed disappointment that his invitation to the archbishop to visit the school had not been accepted. He stated, 'I am as unconvinced by your reasoning as you are unmoved by my representation.'[37] This incident has to be seen in the wider context of Catholic opposition to the Kildare Place Society which resulted in the petition of the Irish bishops to the house of commons in March 1825.

The Royal Hibernian Military School in the Phoenix Park was also in the parish. Originally, it catered for boys and girls. The stated aim of this school was 'the maintaining, educating and apprenticing or placing in our regular army as private soldiers the orphans and children of soldiers in Ireland'.[38] In 1846, changes were made in the constitution of this school.[39] A new charter issued in that year provided that Catholics and Dissenters, at the desire of their parents and guardians were to be exempted from instruction by the Church of Ireland chaplain and from the attendance at the services of the Established Church.[40] Such children were to be allowed to attend their own places of worship and to remain there after the service for religious instruction.[41] The society was also empowered to appoint Catholic priests or Dissenting ministers to visit the school, give religious instruction and perform divine service.[42]

In 1846, girls were no longer admitted to the school which was in future to be exclusively for boys.[43] There were 365 boys in the school at this time including 127 Catholics.[44] Fr Dungan officiated at the new chapel in the school on Palm Sunday, 4 April 1852, on the following two Sundays and on Good Friday.[45] It is not clear whether he was acting in his capacity as chaplain or supplying for the Catholic chaplain. Fr John Leonard, one of Fr Dungan's curates in St Brigid's, was appointed chaplain to the Royal Hibernian Military School in 1859.[46] As officiating Roman Catholic clergyman, he was paid £80 a year and no allowances, that is, he did not have his Sunday breakfast supplied by the school.[47] This figure of £80 was also the annual salary of Alfred Harmsworth, who was then third schoolmaster.[48] Unlike Fr Leonard, Harmsworth had allowances valued at £51. 3s. 4d. a year.[49]

In 1865, Fr Leonard complained to the governors of the school that fourteen open seats for the chapel, included in the parliamentary estimates for 1861, were never provided, despite his repeated applications.[50] He further complained at the 'very wretched accommodation provided for the Catholic clergyman attached to the institution'.[51] His letter, with an accompanying memorandum, was ordered by the House of Commons to be printed as a supplementary return on 30 May 1866. Fr Leonard was named in a house of commons paper 21 August 1861.[52] This time, it was in relation to the case of the children of Private John Murnane, of the 88th Regiment, who died in

Capetown and to the circumstances of Fr Leonard's conversation with one of the children.[53] The question of the religious registration of John and Hugh Murnane having been brought to the notice of the lord lieutenant by Fr Leonard, the governors decided at their meeting on 15 June 1871 that

> his longer continuance as the officiating Roman Catholic clergyman in the Royal Hibernian School is inconsistent with the well-being and proper maintenance of discipline in that institution and that the services of the Revd M. Leonard be dispensed with at the termination of the present quarter.[54]

The parliamentary paper concluded with the correspondence between Cardinal Cullen and Lieutenant Colonel Wynyard.[55] Cardinal Cullen's secretary was asked by the colonel 'to request his Eminence will have the goodness to favour me with the name of the clergyman whom his Eminence may desire should succeed to Fr Leonard'.[56] In reply the cardinal informed the colonel that,

> having read the Revd Dr Leonard's defence, I have been forced to come to the conclusion that the proceedings against him have not established any substantial breach of duty, or want of respect to authority on his part, whilst they do not appear to have been conducted in a form calculated to secure to him that legitimate right of defence which is granted to the lowest of her majesty's subjects.[57]

Despite the cardinal's letters, the governors of the Royal Hibernian School dispensed with the services of Fr John Leonard.[58]

The incident regarding Mr Ellis' school in Abbotstown, the aforementioned affair in the Royal Hibernian School with Fr Leonard, and a controversy in Porterstown which will be referred to later in this chapter, point up the sensitivities relating to proselytism in the parish. While the new National Education Board set up in 1831 sought to establish 'a system of education from which should be banished even the suspicion of proselytism and which, admitting children of all religious persuasions, should not interfere with the peculiar tenets of any',[59] was the ideal, the reality was not always so clear-cut.

Despite these imperfections and the fears they generated, Fr Dean, parish priest of Blanchardstown saw the advantages of the new system and applied in 1832 and 1833 to the National Board for aid for the schools under his care.[60] Not unmindful of the Board's promise 'to look with peculiar favour upon applications proceeding either from a Protestant clergyman and a Roman Catholic clergyman conjointly: a clergyman of the one denomination and a certain number of laymen of the other', Fr Joy Dean sought the support of a number of Protestant laymen.[61] Despite the controversy over Abbotstown school, nine Protestants signed, including factory owners, Thomas Crosthwaite and Benjamin Glorney, and barony cess collector, Richard Phillips.[62] The Revd G. O'Connor, rector of Castleknock refused to sign.[63] Dean's applications were successful and each of the schools taken under the Board was granted ten pounds annually to supplement the teachers' salaries.[64]

This was the position regarding parish schools when Fr Dungan took over in 1836. The provision of so many schools in the parish, considering the poverty of the people, was a great achievement but the numbers attending were probably quite low. The schools at this time were very basic, nothing more than one or two-roomed thatched cabins, poorly lighted and ventilated.[65] An inspector's report described Blanchardstown school in 1836 as wanting flooring, glazing and other repairs but a practically useful school.[66] From his arrival to a year before his death, Fr Dungan was constantly engaged and financially burdened with both the maintenance of the existing schools and the building of new schools at Blanchardstown, Porterstown/Clonsilla and Castleknock. The various expenses involved are recorded in his diary. For example, the floor recommended by the inspector for Blanchardstown boys' school in 1836 was not put in until May 1840 at a cost of 16s. 2½d.[67] On 7 October 1842, Fr Dungan gave a statement of the expenses of the convent girls' school to the prioress, Mrs McOwen – £64. 3s. 7d.[68] The foundation stone of this school had been laid on 24 June 1842.[69] Up to this point, the nuns had run the school in the convent.[70] They were very anxious to have the school separate from the convent so that they could maintain enclosure as much as possible.[71] Each of the nuns said a Hail Mary each day for a new school.[72] This school opened 19 September 1842[73] and became known as the 'Hail Mary School'.[74] It was built beside the Church of St Brigid, and is now used as a community centre. The 'Hail Mary School' had an average attendance of 200 girls in summer and from 50 to 120 in winter.[75]

Porterstown school had a very controversial history. As already mentioned, this school was built by the Protestant owner of Luttrellstown, Luke White and placed under the direction of Fr McPharlan. It was withdrawn on the death of Luke White in 1824.[76] By 1837, Fr Dungan claimed that this school was being used to proselytise Catholic children.[77] Ignatius Callaghan, a Catholic merchant of Fleet Street and Clonsilla, obtained a lease on Porterstown school and it reverted to Catholic management.[78] Fr Dungan put the school under the National Board in 1840.[79] On 17 August 1842, a national schools inspector reported that Henry Garvey, the master of Porterstown school, gave his pupils the following headlines to copy: 'Repeal the Union and relieve your sons' and 'Nature blest Hibernia but English rulers still deceive her'.[80] The National Board did not approve of this and on 25 August they withdrew Garvey's salary.[81] Fr Dungan as manager was informed that the school was to be struck off unless Garvey was removed and a new teacher appointed.[82] Fr Dungan seems to have stood by Garvey and so the school was expelled from the national system.[83] A parish report drawn up by Fr Dungan in 1845 indicates that Garvey was still teaching in Porterstown.[84] The school at this stage had only about twenty children in attendance.[85] Subsequently, on the termination of the lease, the school reverted to the White family of Luttrellstown and Colonel White gave the management of the school to Dr Ralph Sadlier, rector of Castleknock.[86] Dr Sadlier put the school under the National Board in April 1850.[87] As the majority of the children attending the school were Catholics, Dr Sadlier sought the agreement of Fr Dungan, who gave a qualified approval to the school on the understanding that Dr Sadlier would appoint a Catholic master.[88] In the event, Dr Sadlier appointed a Protestant headmaster and a Catholic assistant.[89] The assistant teacher brought the Catholic children to the adjacent Porterstown chapel at 2.30 p.m. each day for religious instruction.[90] This school in Fr Dungan's words 'gave considerable satisfaction to all concerned'.[91]

This 'satisfaction' was short lived and renewed controversy led to the withdrawal of Catholic children from the school in December 1852.[92] The circumstances which led to the withdrawal of the Catholic children only indirectly involved Dr Sadlier. In 1852, according to Fr Dungan, proselytising meetings in which Dr Sadlier's curate was actively involved were held in Castleknock. Porterstown became identified with this through association even though Fr Dungan had the 'highest opinion of Mr Colvin', the Protestant headmaster of Porterstown school.[93] Fr Dungan claimed that Lord Eglington, the lord lieutenant, in the company of Dr Sadlier visited Porterstown school and 'made remarks about Roman Catholics in reference to bibles'. Catholic parents, according to Fr Dungan lost confidence in Dr Sadlier.[94] On 3 January 1853, Fr Dungan set up a school for the Catholic children in Porterstown chapel where they remained until December 1853.[95] The effect of this withdrawal made Porterstown school non-viable. In February 1853, an inspector's report stated that Porterstown National School was closed 'in consequence of the children having been withdrawn to a neighbouring chapel for the purpose of being instructed'.[96] After granting a number of extensions to the school in case the children returned, the Board finally cancelled all aid in 1857.[97] Meanwhile, Fr Dungan had obtained a site of nearly five acres for a new school beside the canal in Porterstown.[98] The Vincentian priests of Castleknock donated this land.[99] On 11 July 1853, the first stone of the new school was laid on the canal bank.[100] The school was built in record time and opened on 15 January 1854 with 58 boys and 66 girls in attendance.[101] The teachers were Timothy Looney and Mrs James Power.[102] This school cost nearly £900 to build and the money was raised through 'local contributions, gratuitous labour and a bequest made to the parish for education'.[103] This three-storey building which is still standing had two large school rooms and two residences; one for the master and monitor, the other for the mistress and monitress. One of the conditions of appointment was that the school principal had to occupy the living quarters as his/her permanent residence.[104] A further condition was that the principal had to give church dues to both Porterstown and Blanchardstown churches.[105]

Fr Dungan applied to the National Board for aid on 24 January 1854.[106] Dr Sadlier objected to the Board granting aid to the new school on the grounds that it 'violated the fundamental principle of the national education system which sought to encourage united education of the various denominations'.[107] Despite this, aid was granted by the Board and that school served that area of the parish for over one hundred years until it was replaced in 1963 by St Mochta's National School in Clonsilla.

In October 1862, Fr Dungan paid £60 for a site for a new school to replace the old thatched school in Castleknock.[108] On Sunday, 17 July 1864, Dr Cullen laid the foundation stone for the Castleknock school.[109] Fr Dungan used the occasion to start a subscription fund for the school and collected a total of £381. 6s. 8d. on the day.[110] In November 1864 he started another collection for the school.[111] By December 1866 he had paid out £704 for materials and labour.[112] On 8 May 1865, teachers and pupils moved into the new school, though the building was not finally completed until 3 July 1867.[113] Fr Dungan drove out that day to see the finished work.[114]

In 1863, John Leckin offered a slated barn in Mulhuddart to replace the existing school.[115] Fr Dungan held a meeting in Mulhuddart on Sunday, 13 September 1863, to collect subscriptions towards fitting out the barn as male and female schools.[116] A total of £65 was promised at the meeting and this enabled Fr Dungan to build chimneys, dash the walls and break doors and windows.[117] When he applied to the National Board for aid on 12 April 1864, he was able to describe the former barn as 'a good substantial slated house, two school rooms plastered and a well dried, even floor'.[118] The school inspector was not quite so impressed and described it as being damp with a floor of clay and lime. The aid was given by the Board.[119]

With the introduction of the national system of education in 1831, the teachers' income was derived from two sources: the National Board's salary and local contributions.[120] In 1835, the board considered £25 a year suitable for teachers.[121] In 1835, the salary of John McLoughlin, master of Blanchardstown school was made up as follows: £10 by the National Board, the children nearly all pay a penny a week, a few being unable to pay, the collection from the children is paid to the parish priest and from it and a collection at a charity sermon in the Roman Catholic chapel, the master receives a salary of £26.[122]

While the salary granted by the Board increased as the century progressed, there was a corresponding tendency for the local contribution to the teacher's salary to decline.[123] Table 1 indicates the funding of the teachers' salaries in 1854.[124] In addition, the teachers in Chapelizod, Clonsilla and Lower Road schools had accommodation provided rent free.[125]

The support of the schools was a continuous drain on finances and a problem for a poor parish such as Blanchardstown. The annual charity sermon was a major fund raising venture for the parish schools throughout Fr Dungan's pastorate. When Cardinal Cullen preached the charity sermon on

Table 1. Teachers' salaries in Blanchardstown parish 1854

School	No. of teachers	Aid granted by Board	Local contribution
Blanchardstown Male	1	£20. 5.0	£10.18.9
Blanchardstown Female	1	£15. 0.0	£ 1. 2.6
Chapelizod Male	1	£20. 0.0	£11. 8.0
Chapelizod Female	1	£20. 5.0	£ 7.14.10
St Brigid's, Castleknock Infants	1	£15. 0.0	£ 7. 2.7
Clonsilla Male	1	£16.13.4	£18. 0.0
Clonsilla Female	1	£ 6.13.4	£10. 0.0
Lower Road	2	£28.10.0	£ 8.14.9
Cabra Convent	2	£28.18.4	Nil

Compiled from figures given in 'History of St Brigid's Church Blanchardstown, 1837–1987'

23 July 1854, the sum of £72. 8s. 1d. was collected.[126] The charity sermons were fashionable occasions. The annual sermon was generally an afternoon function and was well advertised.[127] For example, the charity sermon in September 1863 was advertised before hand in the *Freeman's Journal* and the *Morning News*. In addition 600 circulars were distributed through the post.[128]

Secondary education was also well catered for in the parish, especially by St Vincent's Castleknock. The important role played by the Vincentians in the liturgical and pastoral life of the parish has already been outlined. This connection began in 1835 when the Vincentians opened St Vincent's Ecclesiastical Seminary.[129] Fr John McCann had secured the Castleknock property on 18 October 1834 for £3,600.[130] It had functioned as a school for the sons of Protestant clergy who wished to enter Trinity College,[131] so it was ready for the Vincentians to open their doors to the first students in August 1835. Forty-seven boys had been enrolled in the college in its first year at a fee of 25 guineas each.[132] Very few local students could afford the Castleknock fee of 25 guineas.[133] Of the 711 pupils who attended the college between 1835 and 1859, exactly half were from Dublin.[134] They were mostly the sons of Dublin merchants.[135] One sixth of the pupils were from Leinster, nearly a quarter from Munster, 44 from Ulster and only 19 from Connacht.[136] By 1860 the number of pupils had risen to roughly 100.[137] When St Vincent's College opened in 1835 it became one of 19 second- and third-level colleges in Ireland, there being no firm line between the two at the time.[138] Nor was there a strict division between colleges for lay and for clerical education. Accordingly, what St Vincent's Ecclesiastical Seminary set out to be and what it eventually became were not the same.[139] Publicly, the emphasis was certainly on the ecclesiastical side, but this was for ideological reasons. The community had set out to give parish missions and began conducting such missions in the 1840s.[140] Education of lay pupils, for reasons other than short term, financial expediency, was a departure from that object.[141] However, increasingly, Castleknock became a lay college. Of the 635 pupils who graduated from Castleknock between 1836 and 1861, only 146 or 23 per cent entered Maynooth. Of these, 103 were eventually ordained.[142]

Secondary education for girls was provided by Dominican Convent, Cabra, the Carmelite Convent, Blanchardstown and later the St Joseph of Cluny Sisters who started their school in Blanchardstown in 1859 and transferred to Mount Sackville, still within the parish, in 1861.[143] These secondary schools drew their pupils from a much wider catchment area than Blanchardstown parish. Unlike the National schools, these were no drain on parish finances. In fact, the parish benefited enormously from the more mature Castleknock students who were involved in Sunday catechesis with the children in St Brigid's.[144]

The financing of education in the parish was one of Fr Dungan's major pre-occupations. In his time the National schools were essentially Catholic schools under the management of the parish priest with a large degree of local control. Despite the number of schools provided by the parish and the numbers on rolls, one could not assume that all these children attended regularly. As late as the mid 1880s, parents were regularly reminded by Canon Lynch of the obligation to send their children to school.[145] When Fr Patrick Tynan carried out a census of the parish on 2 June 1897, he estimated that about 16 per cent of the population were illiterate.[146] These adults would have been school-going during the pastorate of Fr Dungan. So, despite the best efforts of Fr Dungan, his committees and all involved in education, there were other socio-economic factors which militated against them and were totally outside their control.

Conclusion

A t the beginning of the nineteenth century Blanchardstown parish was typical of the Catholic Church in Ireland, and was characterized by what Kevin Whelan has described as institutional weakness, an inadequate supply of poor quality churches, insufficient numbers of priests, severe financial difficulties and drastically limited educational facilities.[1] As the century progressed there was a profound transformation. The creation of a new parish structure went hand in hand with the building of new churches.[2] Indeed, the arrival of the 'big chapel' may be taken to signal the transition from both the old folk Catholicism to the new Tridentine form and from the traditional to the modern world.[3] As the main agent of this change Fr Dungan can be seen as the first 'modern' parish priest of Blanchardstown.

The most striking physical monument of this transformation is the church of St Brigid, the new 'big chapel', the spire of which dominates the surrounding landscape. Fr Dungan and his many committees built it over a period of 27 years. It stood as testimony to new pastoral vigour and effective parishioner participation. Many generations of local people have been baptized at the font which Fr Dungan erected and blessed on 15 September 1852.[4] Many of those who were brought for baptism received all the other sacraments in this church and made their final journey there for their funeral service. In times of joy and celebration and in times of sadness and pain, St Brigid's was the place where the people of Blanchardstown gathered. The nineteenth-century parish has now been divided into 12 independent parishes[5] (fig. 5).

The aim of this study has been to describe the Catholic parish of Blanchardstown as seen through the eyes of Fr Dungan. His diary was the main source used and other sources were consulted to corroborate it. Using the diary, the study set out to explore what was normal in the parish rather than what was unique. If this study were done from the perspective of William Rathborne or James Halpin, both contemporaries of the parish priest, or even from the standpoint of one of the Vincentian priests like Thomas McNamara, it would have a different flavour. Another story would be told.

Fr Dungan was the public face of the Catholic Church in Blanchardstown at a time when its confidence was growing. In many ways, what was happening in this parish was typical of what was happening at national level. However, like every other parish it had its own individuality created by the different personalities of priest and people. Blanchardstown was especially fortunate in that priest and people shared a common vision. Because Fr

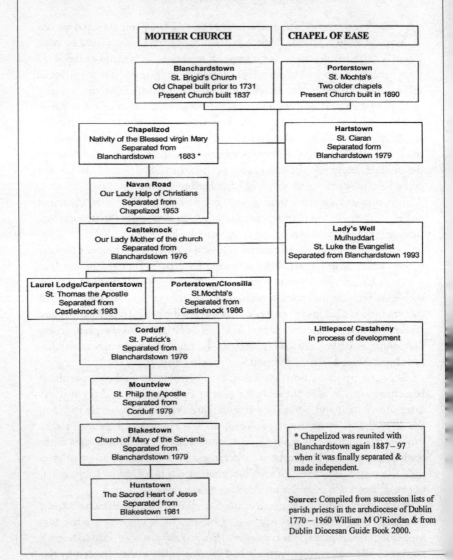

4 The 12 independent parishes constituted from the
mother parish of Blanchardstown.

Dungan's goals were realistic and practical, he received the wholehearted affirmation and co-operation of his parishioners, parishioners who could be discriminating enough to show their disapproval of both Fathers McPharlan and Joy Dean in a public manner.[6] It is characteristic of his pastorate that there is no evidence to suggest any disharmony in the relationship between Fr Dungan and his people in his 32 years in Blanchardstown.

By the time of his death in 1868 all the necessary infrastructure was in place. Liturgical and devotional practices were flourishing. Whether one calls this a 'devotional revolution' or a 'Tridentine evolution,' or something else, the practice of religion in Blanchardstown centred on the parish, the parish priest and the parish church.[7] Is it overstating Fr Dungan's influence to suggest that as his achievements began to be seen and appreciated, 'he was the centre of gravity in the parish, a man who led his community and gave it force and cohesion'?[8]

The parish of course, was not just a functional entity: it was also a symbolic space for the many people who never spent a night outside its confines. It was their complete universe. For them the parish priest incarnated the ultimate authority: an authority that was, so to speak, 'on their side' clearly committed to their best interests and therefore, seen to be 'acceptable', in marked contrast to the civil authority which many of them probably considered alien, oppressive and self-serving. Fr Dungan entered fully into their world as one of them – but one who stood apart. By virtue of his mission and his training he was able to give voice to their heightening expectations. His contribution is best summed up in his death notice which was printed in the *Freeman's Journal*, 7 February 1868:

> His greatest work was the example of a truly Christian life – a light at once to his flock and to his brethren in the sacred ministry. It may be said of him truly, that he was a man simple, upright and fearing God. His people as it ever happens in the case of this soggart aroon, loved, esteemed and venerated and today deplore his loss, in grief bitter in proportion to their love.[9]

Fr Dungan seems to have been a man who had no interest in accumulating worldly possessions. He was prepared to let everything go including his snuff-box and his wrist-watch in the interests of the parish.[10] Not alone did he leave structures in place but he left the parish debt-free.[11] It would have pleased him that the cakes and wine provided after his funeral cost the parish a mere 14s. 9d.[12] If he made a will, no record of it can be found, but the parish account book for 1869 shows that he left £12 to the parish, probably all that he possessed when he died.[13]

The achievement of a parish priest is measured not only by his Christian witness and his preaching the gospel but also by his ability to create the right pastoral structures for his people.[14] On this last point Fr Dungan surely excelled. He was the effective agent of modernization in Blanchardstown and he put in place structures which lasted for the next hundred years. What is striking about this parish priest is his 'enabling role.' He identified the needs of the parish, harnessed the good will of the people and their readiness to co-operate and participate in the programmes conceived by him. His was a strong, active pastoral presence in the parish right up to a few months before his death.

To paraphrase James Kelly, the history of a parish must encompass the laity as well as the clergy.[15] One wonders if Fr Dungan was overly concerned with the building of a 'visible' organization in Blanchardstown? Had he a preoccupation with the institutional Church and its concerns? Were spiritual matters in his hands, always to be 'formalised and 'formulated'? Under him, did everything in the parish have to be reduced to a set of figures which must be balanced? One must further ask was this a personal trait of Fr Dungan's, an institutional characteristic he inherited from Maynooth or a national preoccupation of the parish priest of the mid-nineteenth century? Only comparative studies will enable the historian to explore these questions.

When one considers what was achieved over just three decades in the way of organisational apparatus – confraternities, sodalities – societies, one can only marvel. Yet, the whole system was rather legalistic. There were so many rules and regulations, all of them man-made, every aspect of life covered by precept. The levying of fines on confraternity members for non-attendance at their meetings appears particularly repugnant.[16] The devotional life of the period appears very formal, perhaps, too well regulated, too precise, over-organized and over-externalised. It appears to allow for little in the way of individual divergence or to encourage the development of an 'interior' personal holiness. That the liturgy was in Latin may also have encouraged formalism. However, these are only speculations. It could be said, of course, that this version of Catholicism was adequate to the people's needs at that stage of their spiritual and social development, coming as they were out of a time of spiritual marginalisation and political exclusion.

The diary gives very little insight into the nature of the spirituality of priest or people. Indeed, what is most revealing about it is how little it reveals of the man himself, on either an intellectual or an emotional level. The external is stressed at all times. From the diary, Fr Dungan appears either very reticent and discreet or else unable to express emotion. Was this as a result of the 'rigorist' Maynooth formation of his time or was he so busy with the providing of infrastructure that he lived a relatively 'unreflective' life.

Not only are the intellectual and emotional dimensions missing, but there is no obvious spiritual element either in the diary. Not one line of scripture is quoted or even a phrase from the psalms which he would have recited every day in the Divine Office. He never mentions a book, pious or otherwise, which had nourished him. When he mentions a charity sermon, he notes carefully the venue, the speaker, the amount collected but never the topic or his own or others' response to it. He attends retreats and conferences regularly, but there is no reference to what was discussed. He expresses neither enthusiasm, displeasure nor boredom.

Particularly striking is the contrast between the diary and other contemporary sources, especially those generated by the Carmelite nuns. An example will illustrate. Both Fr Dungan in his diary and the nuns in the convent book acknowledge the generosity of the local people. When James Reilly donated £20 towards plastering St Brigid's Church, a sum four times in excess of what others, including Archbishop Cullen gave, it elicited no response from the parish priest other than the amount recorded.[17] In contrast, when Mrs Ledwidge gave 10*s.* to the nuns after she had been to Mass in the convent, the Mother Prioress was so astonished that she sent a sister out to check if the lady had made a mistake.[18] Again, the nuns record that because of a low hedge around the convent they were 'dreadfully annoyed' that they could be seen and hailed by those passing in the Mail coaches.[19] No doubt, there were many things and possibly, people, who 'dreadfully annoyed' Fr Dungan but the diary does not even hint at irritation. Of course, the convent book gives more than the ordinary female perspective. The writing is coming out of a Carmelite spirituality which depended very much on Divine Providence to supply the everyday needs of the community. They were happy to acknowledge that 'when one source drops off [they] were furnished with another'.[20] On the other hand, Fr Dungan used his committees with their well organised collections to provide for the needs of the parish.

The question still remains, what was the religious experience of the people Fr Dungan served? Were the external structures created without giving them a deeper spiritual significance? Could one lose sight of the true goal and become a 'mere' administrator and activist more committed to external works while overlooking the deeper spiritual realities? Given the needs of the nineteenth-century Church and the level of Christian formation of the laity, is it too great or too idealistic an expectation to look for 'interiority' while at the same time creating the exterior structures?

Perhaps, one is going further than the sources permit. An interesting question which demands further exploration is what was Fr Dungan's purpose in keeping the diary? Was it simply an *aide-mémoire* – a mere noting of events, a memorandum, just a 'desk diary'. If so, one should not expect it to reveal anything of a personal nature. The fact that it had no obvious literary intent, took no heed of parish politics, expressed no prejudices; that it was, in fact, a truly 'factual' account of events, that is its strongest point. For this very reason, the diary has provided the framework and much of the practical detail from which to reconstruct the life of this nineteenth-century parish.

Notes

ABBREVIATIONS

CMD Carmelite Monastery, Drumcondra
DDA Dublin Diocesan Archives
NA National Archives of Ireland
NLI National Library of Ireland
OS Ordnance Survey
PH *A history of St Brigid's Church Blanchardstown, 1837–1987* (Blanchardstown, 1987)

RCB Representative Church Body Library, Rathgar
SBA St Brigid's Parish Archives Blanchardstown, Dublin 15
TCD Trinity College, Dublin
UCD University College, Dublin

INTRODUCTION

1 DDA, Hamilton Papers P1/35/5–6.
2 CMD.
3 Vincentian Archives, St Paul's, Raheny, Dublin 5.
4 DDA, Murray papers, Visitation reports AB3/31/32.
5 SBA, Fr Dungan's diary, entry for 29 Feb. 1852.
6 W.G. Hoskins, *Local history in England* (3rd ed., New York, 1984), p. 46.
7 Ibid.
8 Ibid.
9 James O'Driscoll, *Cnucha, a history of Castleknock* (Dublin, 1977), p. 3.
10 Oral source – the late Fr Séamus McGeehan, parish priest of Blanchardstown, 1 November 1987.
11 Ibid.
12 DDA, Cullen papers, AB4/325/1.
13 *Freeman's Journal*, 7 Feb. 1868, with an obituary in *Freeman's Journal*, 10 Feb. 1868.
14 Inscription on plaque in St Brigid's Church.
15 This plaque was removed when the church extension

was built in 1977. It is now retained in the sacristy of St Brigid's.

1. FR DUNGAN'S BLANCHARDSTOWN

1 R. Gillespie, 'Catholic religious cultures in the diocese of Dublin 1614–97' in J. Kelly and D. Keogh (eds.), *History of the Catholic diocese of Dublin* (Dublin, 1999), p. 136.
2 SBA, Diary inside cover.
3 'A history of St Brigid's Church Blanchardstown, 1837–1987' compiled by Catherine Cullen and Pat Kelly, p. 10. This booklet was presented to parishioners who attended the 150th anniversary Mass, 1 Nov. 1987. (Hereafter referred to as PH)
4 PH, p. 8.
5 Patrick Cunningham, 'The Catholic directory for 1821' in *Reportorium Novum*, 2, no. 2 (1959–60), p. 351.
6–7 Ibid.
8 Ibid., pp 406–33.
9 S.J. Connolly, *Priests and people in pre-famine Ireland* (Dublin, 1982), p. 6. A new

edition of the book was published in 2001.
10 *Freeman's Journal*, 7 Feb. 186? Death announcement of F Dungan.
11 PH, p. 13.
12 *Freeman's Journal*, 7 Feb. 1868
13 DDA, Murray papers AB3/30/9–11.
14 Ibid.
15 W.M. O'Riordan, 'Successio lists of parish priests in the archdiocese of Dublin, 1771 1960' in *Reportorium Novum* 3, no. 1 (1962), p. 178.
16 PH, p. 7.
17 W.M. O'Riordan, 'The succession of parish priests the archdiocese of Dublin 1771–1851' in *Reportorium Novum*, i, no. 2 (1956), p. 42
18 Ibid.
19 *The history of St Mary of the Isle and the story of the Catho Church in Douglas* (Douglas 1984), p. 11.
20 Metropolitan Cathedral Christ the King, Liverpo Archdiocesan Archive, PB/ Correspondence between Jo Joseph Gallagher, R.C. Cha House, Douglas to Right Re Dr Brown, Vicar Apostolic Northern District 1840–18

60

21 Ibid.
22 DDA, Murray papers, AB3/30/9–11.
23 Ibid.
24 CMD, Convent book, p. 3.
25 SBA Note on back of account book for 1839.
26 PH, p. 11.
27 Vincentian Archive Raheny, Thomas McNamara, 'Memoirs of the Congregation of the Mission, England, Ireland, Scotland, 1835–67', (MS), p. 66.
28 *Freeman's Journal*, 4 August 1836.
29 SBA, Diary, inside cover.
30 Evidence gathered from examination of diary and account books, where the names occur very frequently. They will be individually footnoted as they are referred to in the course of this study.
31 H.P.R. Finberg, *The local historian and his theme* (Leicester 1965), p. 5.
32 PH, p. 32.
33 Ibid.
34 DDA, Murray papers, Visitation report, 1836, AB3/31/7.
35–36 Ibid.
37 SBA, Account book, 1868. CMD, Convent book, p. 3.
38–40 Ibid., p.20. Oral source, Sister Immaculata, Prioress, Monastery of the Incarnation, Hampton, 8 Dec. 2000. CMD, Convent book, p. 32. Ibid., pp 26–30. *Dominican Sisters, Cabra, 1819–1994, celebrating 175 years* (Dublin, 1994), p. 3. *St Mary's School for Deaf Girls 1846–1996* (Dublin, 1996), p. 11. Ibid. J.H. Murphy (ed.), *Nos autem, Castleknock College, its contribution* (Dublin, 1996), p. 9. PH, p. 11. SBA, Parish inventory, conducted by Fr Tynan, 1898.
–52 NLI, *Census of Ireland 1851*, Co. of Dublin, for the barony of Castleknock, pp 23, 24.

53–56 DDA, Hamilton papers, , PI 35/5–6.
57 *History of the parish of Donabate* (Dublin, 1988), p. 11.
58–63 DDA, Hamilton papers, PI 35/5–6.
64 *Freeman's Journal*, Fr Dungan's death notice, 7 Feb. 1868.
65 SBA, Note in (parish) account book Sept. 1868 of payment of 2s. to Betty for the repair of blankets.
66 SBA, Account book, 1836.
67 PH, p. 13.
68 SBA, Diary, inside cover.
69 PH, p. 13.
70–72 SBA, Entries in parish account books.
73 SBA, Confraternity books.
74 Fr Dungan's homily at first Mass in St Brigid's, 13 Oct. 1837, printed in *Blanchardstown Chronicle*, 'The story of a community from Celtic times to the present', p. 29.
75 SBA, The Confraternity of the Christian Doctrine book.
76 Griffith's valuation for Ashtown and Blanchardstown, 1852.
77 SBA, Parish account books, 1845–68.
78 *Freeman's Journal*, Obituary, 10 Feb. 1868.
79 Lieutenant Joseph Archer, *Statistical Survey Co. Dublin* (Dublin, 1801), p. 4.
80 John O'Donovan, *Ordnance Survey name books*, Dublin county, (no. 47) vol. 1.
81 *Census of Ireland 1851*, County of Dublin, pp 23, 24.
82 Ibid.
83–88 Poor Law Inquiry (Ireland) 1836, H.C. xxxiii, Appendix D1. Reply to questionnaire.
89 SBA, Diary, Poor List, 9 Jan. 1852 to 12 Dec. 1866.
90–92 SBA, Diary entry, 9 Jan. 1858.
93 Ibid., entry 12 Jan. 1852.
94 NA, Cholera papers, 1831, application forms for relief for the Civil Parish of Castleknock.
95 *Freeman's Journal*, Fr Dungan's death notice, 7 Feb. 1868.

96 *Census of Ireland 1851*, County of Dublin.
97 SBA, References to occupations in parish registers.
98 Reply to questionnaire, *Poor Law Inquiry*.
99 SBA, References to parish registers.
100 Griffith's valuation for Blanchardstown, 1852.
101 Griffith's valuation for Ashtown, 1852.
102–103 Griffith's valuation for Pellets-town, 1852.
104–105 O'Driscoll, *Cnucha*, p. 90.
106–107 Bernard Neary, *The candle factory: five hundred years of Rathbornes, master chandlers* (Dublin, 1998), p. 34
108 SBA, Parish account books.
109 SBA, Diary.
110 Connolly, *Priests and people in pre-Famine Ireland*, p. 15.
111 SBA, Diary entry.
112–114 RCB Library, Vestry minutes 1806–1870, Civil parish of Castleknock, P352/35/3.
115–117 *Census of Ireland 1851*, County of Dublin. Comparison of census figures for 1841–1851.
118 PH, p. 31.
119 NA, Dispensary report, Castleknock Dispensary, 1833.
120 SBA, Parish account book, 1849.
121 SBA, Diary entry, 10 June 1844.
122 Ibid., 10 Feb. 1845.
123 Ibid., 1 June 1841.
124–125 Ibid., 25 Nov. 1845.
126 Ruth Delaney, *Ireland's Royal Canal, 1789–1992* (Dublin, 1992), p. 92.
127 SBA, Diary, 30 July 1856.
128–129 Ibid., 18 July 1851.
130–131 Ibid., 19 June 1856.
131 Ibid.
132 Ibid., 30 July 1856.
133 Ibid., 10 Oct. 1856.
134 Ibid., Dec. (no specific date).
135–137 Ibid., 8 Dec. 1845.
138–139 Ibid., 30 Nov. 1845.
140 Fingal County Council Archives, Turnpike Trust Records.

141   SBA, Diary, references throughout.
142   Ibid., 15 Aug. 1845.
143   Ibid., 10 June 1846.
144   CMD, Convent book, p. 22.
145   SBA, Diary entry, 26 Nov. 1845.
146–147   Ibid., 1 July 1846.
148   Ibid., 13 May 1856.
149   SBA, Parish account book, 1845.
150–152   Ibid., 1 Jan. 1857.
153   SBA, Parish account book, 1858.
154   SBA, Newspaper cutting in Diary.
155–156   SBA, Diary entry, 9 June 1853.
157–158   SBA, Parish account book, 1858.
159   Ibid., 6 Aug. 1845.
160   Ibid., 29 Dec. 1845.
161   Ibid., 20 Jan. 1855.
162   Ibid., 14 Feb. 1855.
163   Ibid., 16 Feb. 1855.
164   Ibid., 15 March 1855.
165   Ibid., 21 March 1857.
166   Ibid., 20 April 1858.
167   Ibid., 9 Jan. 1856.
168   Ibid., 21 Oct. 1853.
169   Ibid., 6 June 1854.
170–171   Sean P. Farragher, *Père Leman: educator and missionary 1826–1880, founder of Blackrock College, Co. Dublin* (Dublin, 1988), p. 95.
172   Ibid., p. 96.
173–175   Ibid., p. 95.
176–179   Ibid., p. 97.
180   Ibid., p. 151.
181   Ibid., p. 155.
182   Sr Calixta's papers, Mount Sackville, quoted in PH, p. 16.
183   Ibid.
184   PH, p. 49.
185–189   SBA, Parish account book, Nov. 1854.
190–192   PH, p. 19.
193   Ibid., p. 20.
194–195   Donal Kerr, 'Dublin's forgotten archbishop, Daniel Murray, 1768–1852' in J. Kelly and D. Keogh (eds.), *History of the Catholic diocese of Dublin* (Dublin, 2000), p. 259.
196–198   DDA, Murray papers, AB3/32/4.

199–200   NLI, MS 331–5, The Blanchardstown Affair, July 1848 and other political subjects.
201   SBA, Diary entry, 13 July 1852.
202–203   Ibid., 22 July 1852.

2.   A CHURCH IN TRANSITION

1–3   DDA, Murray papers, Visitation report 1831, AB3/31/2.
4–6   PH, p. 13.
7–8   Ibid., p. 14.
9   SBA, Parish account book 1859–68.
10–11   PH, p. 14.
12–13   SBA, Diary entry, 14 Sept. 1844.
14   Ibid., entry 20 August 1845.
15   PH, p. 14.
16   Griffith's Valuation for Chapelizod, 1852.
17–19   SBA, Parish account book, 1844–52.
20   SBA, Diary entry, 15 August 1854.
21   Ibid., entry 11 March 1854.
22   Ibid., entry 22 July 1855.
23–26   SBA, Book of leases and inventories drawn up by Fr O'Donovan P.P. St Brigid's 1879.
27–40   SBA, Parish account book 1856.
41   SBA, Diary entry, 20 Sept. 1857.
42   SBA, Parish account book 1856–68.
43   SBA, Diary entry, 4 Jan. 1863.
44   SBA, Parish account book., 1856–68.
45   PH, p. 15.
46   SBA, Diary entry, 1 Oct. 1863.
47   *Freeman's Journal*, 18 August 1863.
48–49   PH, p. 16.
50   SBA, Diary entry, 17 April 1852.
51   Ibid., 31 August 1856.
52   SBA, Parish account book, 1859.
53   Cunningham, 'Catholic Directory 1821', p. 406.
54–56   DDA, Murray papers, AB3/31/2.

57   Dáire Keogh, '"the pattern of the flock": John Thomas Troy 1786–1823' in Kelly and Keogh (eds), *History of the diocese of Dublin*, p. 227.
58   Ibid., p. 228.
59–60   McNamara, 'Memoirs of the Congregation', p. 66.
61–62   Ibid., p. 68.
63   Canon Sheehan, *My new curate* (9th ed., Dublin, 1952) p. 236.
64   Connolly, *Priests and people in pre-Famine Ireland*, p. 78.
65   SBA, Newspaper cutting entitled 'Regularity of habit' in Diary.
66   SBA, Newspaper cutting, 'The cheerful wife' in Diary
67–73   DDA, Murray papers, AB3/32/4.
74   SBA, Confraternity book.
75   DDA, Murray papers, Visitation report, AB3/31/7
76   SBA, Confraternity book.
77   M. Brennan, 'The Confraternity of Christian Doctrine in Ireland', in *Irish Ecclesiastical Record* xliii (1934), pp 560–77.
78   DDA, Murray papers, Visitation report, AB3/31/7
79   Ibid.
80–101   SBA, Confraternity book listing members for 1844.
102   SBA, Parish account book 1856–68.
103–107   SBA, Confraternity book.
108   Keogh, 'The pattern of the flock': John Thomas Troy, 1786–1823' p. 230.
109   SBA, Confraternity book.
110   Keogh, 249.
111   NA, Cholera papers, 1832
112   PH, p. 26.
113   DDA, Murray papers, AB3/31/2.
114–115   SBA, Confraternity book.
116–117   SBA, recorded by Fr J Dean on back page of account book for 1829.
118–120   Rev Philip Deane OFM, Multyfarnham, 8 Dec. 2000, oral source.
121   PH, p. 10.

122 SBA, Diary entry, 13 August
     1850.
123–124 Ibid., entry undated.
125 Ibid.
126–127 SBA, Parish account
     book 1856–68.
128 SBA, Diary entry, 6 August
     1855.
129 Ibid., 1 Feb. 1862.
130–134 Ibid., 1 Feb. 1865.
135–137 SBA, account books.
138–140 SBA, Parish account
     book, 1856–68.
141 SBA, Diary entry, 1 Oct. 1863.
142 Ibid., 11 Nov. 1866.
143–147 SBA, Parish account
     book, 1856–68.
148 Murphy (ed.), Nos autem, p.
     12.
149 McNamara, 'Memoirs of the
     congregation', p. 166.
150 PH, p. 10.
151 SBA, Parish account book,
     1856–68.
152 PH, p. 12.
153–156 SBA, Parish account
     book, 1856–68.
157–158 Miles Ronan, An apostle
     of Catholic Dublin, Father
     Henry Young (Dublin, 1944),
     p. 90.
159–161 PH, p. 24.
162–164 SBA, Parish account
     book. Record of £60
     collected.
165 SBA, Diary entry, 6 Nov. 1853.
166–168 SBA, Parish account
     book, 1856–68.
169 DDA, Murray papers,
     Visitation report, AB3/31//2.
170 CMD, Convent book, p. 18.
171 SBA, Parish account book,
     Dec. 1849.
172–173 PH, p. 61.
174 R. Gillespie and M. Hill
     (eds.), Doing Irish local history:
     pursuit and practice (Belfast,
     1998), p. 20.
175 R. Gillespie, The sacred in the
     secular; religious change in
     Catholic Ireland 1500–1700
     (Vermont, 1993), p. 16.
176 J. Kelly, 'The impact of the
     penal laws' in Keogh and
     Kelly (eds.), History of the
     Catholic diocese of Dublin, p.
     165.

177–178 D. Keogh, 'Daniel
     Murray, 1768–1852',
     p. 229.
179 R. Gillespie, Devoted people,
     belief and religion in early
     modern Ireland (Manchester,
     1997), p. 92.
180 R. Gillespie, Doing local
     history, p. 20.
181 C. Ó Danachair, 'The holy
     wells of County Dublin' in
     Reportorium Novum, 2, no. 1,
     1957–8.
182–183 Kelly, 'The impact of the
     penal laws' in Keogh and
     Kelly (eds), History of the
     Catholic diocese of Dublin, p.
     165.
184–185 PH, p. 46.
186 Austin Cooper, 'A journey
     from Dublin to the shores of
     Lough Derg, 1741' in Journal
     of the Royal Society of
     Antiquaries of Ireland, xxii
     (1892), p. 15.
187 Ordnance Survey Name Books,
     Dublin county, (no. 47), vol 1.
188 M.V. Ronan, 'Mulhuddart
     and Cloghran – Hiddert' in
     Journal of the Royal Society of
     Antiquaries of Ireland, lxx
     (1940).
189 Ibid.
190–193 PH, p. 47.
194–195 Quoted in Cooper,
     'Journey from Dublin to
     Lough Derg', p. 15.
196 PH, p. 46.
197 Faulkners Dublin Journal, 15
     August 1754.
198 Samuel Lewis, A topographical
     dictionary of Ireland (3 vols
     London, 1837), i, p.23.
199 SBA, Diary entry, 15 August
     1852.
200 UCD Folklore Commission,
     Blanchardstown file.
201 DDA, Murray papers,
     Pastoral letter, AB3/331/2.
202 SBA, Confraternity book
     which includes Purgatorian
     Society book.
203 R. Gillespie, 'Catholic
     religious cultures 1614–1697'
     in Keogh and Kelly (eds.),
     History of the Catholic diocese
     of Dublin, p. 137.

204 Visitation report, 1831,
     DDA, Murray papers,
     AB3/31/2.

3. THE PROVISION OF
EDUCATION IN THE PARISH
OF BLANCHARDSTOWN

1 William Carleton, in Irish
   Penny Journal, December 1840.
2 P.J. Corish, A history of Irish
   Catholicism (Dublin, 1967), v,
   p. 5.
3–4 Ibid., p. 12.
5 Ibid., p. 6.
6–8 Ibid., p. 13.
9 Ibid., p. 12.
10–15 Second Report of the
   Commissioners of Irish
   Education Inquiry, H.C. 1826
   (12) xii, 1.
16 CMD, Convent book,
   Hampton, p. 6.
17–18 Second Report of the
   Commissioners of Irish
   Education inquiry, H.C. 1826
   (12) xii, 1.
19–20 PH, P. 37.
21–23 Ibid., p. 27.
24 Patrick Cunningham, 'The
   Catholic Directory for 1821'
   in Reportorium Novum, 2, no. 2
   (1959–60), p. 351.
25–29 Catholic registry and almanac
   (Dublin, 1836), pp 162–3.
30–32 PH, p. 28.
33–37 DDA, Murray
   correspondence, AB3/35/69.
38–44 Michael Quane, The Royal
   Hibernian Military School
   Phoenix Park Dublin', in
   Dublin Historical Record, xviii,
   (1962–3), p. 45.
45 SBA, Diary entry, 4 April 1852.
46–51 Quane, 'The Royal
   Hibernian Military School',
   p. 51.
52–57 Quoted in Quane, 'The
   Royal Hibernian Military
   School', p. 51.
58 Ibid., p. 52.
59 Corish, History of Irish
   Catholicism, v, p. 6.
60–62 NA, Initial application,
   ED1/28 No. 39.
63–64 PH, p. 30.
65 Ibid., p. 28.

66 Inspector's Report for Blanchardstown village national school 1836, quoted in PH, p.31.
67 SBA, Parish account book, 1842.
68 SBA, Diary entry, 7 Oct. 1842.
69 Ibid., 24 June 1842.
70–71 CMD Convent book, p. 16.
72 Sister Immaculata, Prioress CMD Oral source, 14 Nov. 2000.
73 SBA, Diary, 19 Sept. 1842.
74 Sr Immaculata, CMD Oral source.
75 CMD Convent book, p. 17.
76–78 PH, p. 32.
78 Ibid.
79 NA, ED 1/28 10.95.
80–83 PH, p. 47.
84–86 SBA, Parish account book 1845.
87 NA, ED 1/29 No. 49.
88–89 PH, p. 33.
89 Ibid.
90 SBA, Diary entry, 3 Jan. 1853.
91 Ibid., 15 Jan. 1854.
92–94 DDA, Cullen papers, AB4/325/1. Memorial of the people of Blanchardstown.
95 SBA, Diary entry, undated.
96 PH, p. 34.
97 Ibid., p. 29.
98 PH, p.34.
99 Fr Myles Reardon CM, Maynooth. Oral source, Nov. 2000.
100–102 SBA, Diary entry, 11 Jan. 1853.
103 SBA, Parish account book, 1856–68.
104–105 PH, p. 31.
106 NA, ED 1/29 No. 128.
107 PH, p. 31.
108 SBA, Parish account book, 1856–68.

109 SBA, Diary entry, 17 July 1864.
110–112 SBA, Parish account book, 1856–68.
113–114 SBA, Diary entry, 3 July 1867.
115 Ibid., 13 September 1863.
116–117 ISBA, Parish account book, 1856–68.
118 NA, ED 1/30, No 104.
119 PH, p. 31.
120 Ibid., p. 37.
121–122 Ibid., p. 31.
123 Ibid., p. 37.
124 Compiled from figures given in PH, p. 37.
125 PH, p. 38.
126 SBA, Diary entry. 23 July 1854.
127 *Freeman's Journal*, 18 July 1854.
128 SBA, Parish account book, 1856–68.
129 Murphy, *Nos Autem*, p. 9.
130–132 Ibid., p. 10.
133 Ibid., p. 12.
134–135 Ibid., p. 13.
136–142 Ibid., p. 15.
143 PH, p. 39.
144 SBA, Confraternity book, St Brigid's Archives.
145 SBA, Altar book, 1884.
146 SBA, Inventory book.

CONCLUSION

1–3 K. Whelan in 'The Catholic parish, the Catholic chapel and village development in Ireland' in *Irish Geography*, xvi (1983), p. 2.
4 SBA, Diary entry, 15 Sept. 1852.
5 Compiled from Dublin Diocesan Guidebook 2000. As is to be expected, the diocesan priests have

responsibility for many of these new parishes. The regular orders have accepted responsibility for others; the Pallotines for Corduff parish; the Servites for Blakestown parish; the Capuchins for the two oratories in Blanchardstown village and in the Town Centre; the Passionists for the parish of Littlepace/Castaheany, which is in the process of being cut off from Blanchardstown. The Camillians work as chaplains in the James Connolly Hospital, Blanchardstown.
6 DDA, Murray papers, AB3/30/9.
7 P.J. Corish (ed.), *A history of Irish Catholicism*, v (Dublin, 1970), quoted by K. Whelan in 'The Catholic parish'.
8 Whelan 'The Catholic parish' p. 12 quoting 'Tarry Flynn' by Patrick Kavanagh.
9 *Freeman's Journal*, 7 Feb. 1868
10 SBA, Parish account book, 1856–68.
11 SBA, Parish account book, 1863.
12 SBA, Parish account book, 1868.
13 SBA, Parish account book 1869.
14 Kerr, 'Dublin's forgotten archbishop, Daniel Murray, 1768–1852', p. 247.
15 J. Kelly, 'The historiography of the diocese of Dublin' in Kelly and Keogh (eds.), *History of the Catholic diocese Dublin*, p. 8.
16 SBA, Confraternity book.
17 SBA, Diary entry, 1 June 185
18 CMD, Convent book, p. 18.
19 Ibid., p. 2.
20 Ibid., p. 18.